THE LIFE OF A SONG
VOLUME 2

THE LIFE OF A SONG VOLUME 2

The stories behind 50 more of
the world's best-loved songs

EDITED BY DAVID CHEAL
AND JAN DALLEY

FINANCIAL
TIMES

BREWER'S

First published in Great Britain in 2018 by Brewer's, an imprint of Chambers Publishing Limited. An Hachette UK company.

This edition published in 2018 by Chambers Publishing Limited.

Brewer's® is a registered trademark of Chambers Publishing Limited.

Copyright © *Financial Times* 2018

The right of *Financial Times* to be identified as the Author of the Work has been asserted by it in accordance with the Copyright, Designs and Patents Act 1988.

Database right Chambers Publishing Limited (makers).

British Library Cataloguing in Publication Data:
a catalogue record for this title is available from the British Library.

Library of Congress Catalog Card Number: on file.

ISBN: 978 1 473 66827 0
eISBN: 978 1 473 66826 3

1

The publisher has used its best endeavours to ensure that any website addresses referred to in this book are correct and active at the time of going to press. However, the publisher and the author have no responsibility for the websites and can make no guarantee that a site will remain live or that the content will remain relevant, decent or appropriate.

The publisher has made every effort to mark as such all words which it believes to be trademarks. The publisher should also like to make it clear that the presence of a word in the book, whether marked or unmarked, in no way affects its legal status as a trademark.

Every reasonable effort has been made by the publisher to trace the copyright holders of material in this book. Any errors or omissions should be notified in writing to the publisher, who will endeavour to rectify the situation for any reprints and future editions.

Typeset in Celeste & Anodyne by Palimpsest Book Production Ltd, Falkirk, Stirlingshire
Printed and bound in Great Britain by Clays Ltd, Elcograf S.p.A.

Chambers Publishing Limited policy is to use papers that are natural, renewable and recyclable products and made from wood grown in sustainable forests. The logging and manufacturing processes are expected to conform to the environmental regulations of the country of origin.

Carmelite House
50 Victoria Embankment
London EC4Y 0DZ
www.chambers.co.uk

CONTENTS

INTRODUCTION

What is a song? Music and words tell a story, convey an emotion, conjure up images. Songs have been doing this for centuries, although the popular song as we know it today in the West, with its verses and choruses and often romantic lyrics, is directly descended from the lovelorn ballads that were toured around Europe by medieval troubadours, who were in turn influenced by the music of Islamic Spain.

But songs are more than verses and choruses and melodies. A song is a mystery. It has a unique ability to summon up memories, to bind people together, to make us tingle with pleasure. It can move us, and it can make us move. Neurologists have found that listening to a song, with music and lyrics and rhythm, affects many different parts of the brain, fizzing out into all four of its lobes and connecting them to create an experience that is like no other. It's like going on a journey – but sometimes the world seems to stop. It can summon up the past; yet songs are always moving forward. There is nothing else like it – a synthesis of words and music whose impact is both cerebral and physical.

And something else happens, in addition to all of this, when a song is taken on and adapted by a new 'voice'. A song that has become strongly associated with a particular singer or group – often, these days, the people who wrote it – takes on new resonances; sometimes we as listeners are shocked. Sometimes, it doesn't seem right. Sometimes, though, it works – it sings, and the song takes on a new life.

Which brings us to the contents of this book. Like its predecessor, *The Life of a Song Volume 2* is a compilation of columns that have appeared in *FT Weekend*. Each chapter tells the story of a well-known song, unearthing its archaeology, its biography, its descendants. The songs here range in style from pure pop to primal rock'n'roll, from crunching blues-rock to swirling psychedelia. Some date back to the nineteenth century, such as 'O Sole Mio', which began life as a Neapolitan ballad and became a hit in the hands of Elvis Presley as 'It's Now or Never'. This is also one of three songs in these pages that have become popular on the football terraces of Britain, and elsewhere – the others being The White Stripes' 'Seven Nation Army', whose riff became globally adopted as a wordless chant, and 'You'll Never Walk Alone', which started out as a hymnal number in the Rodgers and Hammerstein musical *Carousel*.

Some songs have transcended genres: 'Time After Time', a hit for thrift-store icon Cyndi Lauper in 1983, became a staple in the repertoire of Miles Davis. Some, such as 'Greensleeves', have mysterious histories; though it's widely believed to have been written by Henry VIII, this is almost certainly a myth. Some were revised by their songwriters before recording: if The Kinks' 'Waterloo Sunset' had been released under its original title, 'Liverpool Sunset', would it have had the same impact? There are gleaming factoid-nuggets such as these scattered throughout the 50 stories that make up this book. It's a book to dip into, offering bite-sized essays that inform and entertain, and will send readers scurrying back to listen to these songs in all their beauty and mystery.

CONTRIBUTORS

Peter Aspden

Peter Aspden is a former arts editor and writer for the *Financial Times*. He was brought up in Washington DC where he bought his first plastic Beatles wig to sing 'I Want to Hold Your Hand' in front of the mirror. He studied Philosophy, Politics and Economics at St Edmund Hall, Oxford, where he thought that Californian soft rock would change the world. He has written about sport, books, travel and the arts for a wide variety of publications. He is currently thinking about writing a book, but has been sidetracked trying to work out the guitar chords of 'God Only Knows'.

Helen Barrett

Helen Barrett is based in London and is the *FT*'s work and careers editor, where she writes about leadership, management, entrepreneurship and business education. She spends far too much time reading and thinking about – and listening to – pop music.

Helen Brown

Helen Brown is an arts journalist whose articles have appeared in the *Financial Times*, the *Daily Telegraph*, the *Independent*, the *Guardian* online, the *New Statesman* and *The Spectator*. Highlights of her interviewing career have included a lesson in playing the guitar with acrylic nails from Dolly Parton, bird-watching with Amy Winehouse and scouring corner shops for fine wines with Grace Jones. She lives in Essex with her two small children and too much vinyl.

David Cheal

David Cheal has been reviewing music since the early 1980s, and was a pop critic for the *Daily Telegraph* for 20 years. He now works on the *Financial Times* arts pages, where he writes and commissions the weekly 'Life of a Song' column and also contributes reviews and features. When he was growing up, he wanted to be Jack Bruce but never got round to learning how to play the bass.

Richard Clayton

After a decade and more of mainly music freelancing for the *The Sunday Times* and the *Financial Times*, Richard Clayton swapped tinnitus for timetables to retrain as an English teacher. He remembers interviewing Amy Winehouse over bacon and eggs, and small talk about cycling with Jakob Dylan. Proud to have been an early adopter of Wild Beasts, Kendrick Lamar and Father John Misty, he still hopes to write during the summer holidays.

Jon Dennis

Jon Dennis has written, podcasted and made videos for the *Financial Times*, the *Guardian*, the *Mail on Sunday*, *NME* and *Word*. In his previous incarnation as a musician in the 1980s and '90s, his band supported Radiohead. Jon is an insatiable collector of vinyl records, and if anyone has a spare first pressing of David Bowie's debut album on the Deram label, please let him know. Jon is currently writing a bestselling book and developing a hit podcast about music.

Dan Einav

Dan Einav is an arts writer whose work has appeared in the *Financial Times, Little White Lies, Monocle* and the *i* newspaper. He went to a school in Cambridge which may or may not have partially inspired Pink Floyd's 'Another Brick in the Wall' and now lives in London just down the road from a pub where a young Jimi Hendrix used to perform. Despite still vaguely entertaining hopes of headlining Glastonbury, he is only the third-best guitarist in his household.

Harriet Fitch Little

Harriet Fitch Little is an arts writer and interviewer for the *Financial Times*, and the deputy editor of *Kinfolk* magazine. Her niche obsession with Lebanese funk and south-east Asian psychedelic rock is the result of years spent on the desks of various obscure foreign newspapers.

Alison Gunn

After studying performing arts at Middlesex Polytechnic, Alison Gunn trod the boards for 15 years, appearing in touring shows such as *Chicago* and *Sweet Charity*, and at the Edinburgh Festival with comedy groups Newsrevue and The Flatlettes. She moved into journalism and has worked as a subeditor and writer on numerous magazines and newspapers, including *The Sunday Times*, the *FT*'s *How to Spend It*, *ES Magazine* and the *Financial Times* arts pages. She lives in south-east London with her husband, son and family cat, and enjoys going to the ballet, playing saxophone with a local big band and learning Russian.

Michael Hann

Michael Hann is a freelance writer, formerly music editor of the *Guardian* and editor of *FourFourTwo*. He bores on about Bruce Springsteen and The Hold Steady at any opportunity, and once – inadvertently – spat a mouthful of half-chewed doner kebab on to the arm of the drummer of Secret Machines.

Mike Hobart

Mike Hobart is the *Financial Times* jazz critic. He was a full-time musician for many years and still plays tenor sax. He now leads his own jazz quintet, whose CD *Evidential* was released in 2016 through anotherworldmusic.

David Honigmann

Building on his misspent youth browsing in Sterns Records, pursuing an interest founded on his parents' copy of 'Missa Luba', David Honigmann is now world music critic for the *Financial Times*. He was also a contributor to the *Rough Guide Book of Playlists*, and is the co-author of a range of children's books. He has only missed one WOMAD this century.

Ludovic Hunter-Tilney

Ludovic Hunter-Tilney is the *Financial Times* pop critic and has also written for the *Guardian*, *The Sunday Times* and the *New Statesman*. In 2014 he won the London Press Club's arts reviewer of the year award. He lives in London.

Ian McCann

Ian McCann is a freelance journalist and the former editor of *Record Collector* magazine. He has written for *NME*, *Q* and the *Independent*, and worked as a reporter on BBC Radio 1. An obsessive accumulator of vinyl, he is a big fan of soul, jazz and reggae, and owns a hi-fi system so loud that it's like the nuclear deterrent: let's hope it will never be used.

Sue Norris

Sue Norris is a former associate editor of the *FT Weekend* magazine and is now a freelance writer and editor. Sue grew up on American soul and funk, and once thought nothing of spending a day's wages on an American import from Contempo Records in London's Hanway Street. She still spends rather too much time watching old episodes of *Soul Train*.

Jude Rogers

Jude Rogers has been a journalist, arts critic, reviewer, interviewer and comment writer for nearly 15 years for the *Guardian*, *The Observer*, *The Sunday Times*, the *Independent*, the *Daily Telegraph*, *Radio Times*, the *New Statesman*, *Marie Claire*, *Cosmopolitan*, *Red*, *In-Style* and *The Pool* – and has been delighted to start writing for the *Financial Times*. She has made documentaries for Radio 4, and has judged many music prizes, including the Mercury for six years.

Paul Sexton

Music writer and broadcaster Paul Sexton contributes to the *Financial Times*, *The Sunday Times*, *Billboard*, *Music Week* and Universal Music's global website uDiscovermusic. He presents and produces documentaries and other programmes for BBC Radio 2 and shows for such airlines as Virgin Atlantic, Emirates and KLM. He started writing for the now-lamented weekly music press while still at school, for *Record Mirror*. Forty years later, as he continues to wait to be told to get a proper job, his wide-ranging tastes also see him contributing to such magazines as *Country Music* and *Prog*.

Fiona Sturges
Fiona Sturges is a writer and journalist who specializes in music and popular culture. For 20 years she worked as an interviewer and reviewer for the *Independent*. She is now an arts columnist for the *Financial Times* and the *Guardian*, and lectures in Popular Music Journalism at Southampton Solent University.

I'M A BELIEVER

In 1965 an advertisement appeared in US publications *Daily Variety* and the *Hollywood Reporter*: 'Madness!! Auditions. Folk & Roll Musicians–Singers for acting roles in new TV series. Running Parts for 4 insane boys, age 17–21.'

From these auditions emerged The Monkees, four young men whose records would, for a while, outsell the combined might of The Beatles and The Rolling Stones. In an age of singer–songwriters, artistic credibility and emotional authenticity, The Monkees were unashamedly plastic, the original manufactured boy band.

Their first single, 'Last Train to Clarksville', written by Tommy Boyce and Bobby Hart, reached Number 1 in the US. Its follow-up, 'I'm a Believer', was the work of a young New York songwriter-for-hire, Neil Diamond, who had initially tried to place it with country singer Eddie Arnold, as well as recording it himself. With its nifty guitar intro, catchy keyboard riff (all played by session musicians) and upbeat chorus, the song was an instant hit for The Monkees in 1966; Diamond also had some success the following year with his own version of the song, whose appeal lies in its irresistibly innocent, romantic, epiphanic chorus. The Monkees, meanwhile, fought back against the corporate machine and eventually got to play and write their own material, culminating in a strange but

sporadically entertaining 1969 concept album called *The Monkees Present.*

Fast-forward to the early 1970s. Robert Wyatt, an English musician, was making a name as drummer with a proggy, jazzy outfit called Soft Machine. Then, in 1973, at a party in London, Wyatt fell out of a fourth-floor window and was paralysed from the waist down. Drumming, clearly, was now too physically challenging, so he announced his return to the music scene the following year as a singer, with his totally unexpected rendition of 'I'm a Believer'. Wyatt's 1974 appearance on the BBC's *Top of the Pops* is one of the show's great unforgettable 'moments'. The programme's producers had tried to persuade him out of his wheelchair and into a regular chair; he refused, and there he sat, rocking gently from side to side, his frail voice and his London accent bringing new meaning and emotional depth to the song's lyric: here was a man, the song said, who believed in life. (His band on *Top of the Pops*, incidentally, included Pink Floyd's Nick Mason on drums and Andy Summers, later of The Police, on acoustic guitar.)

Wyatt's version was a triumph, and showed that it was not always essential to have written a song for it to be authentic, personal and emotional. But to anyone under the age of 30, 'I'm a Believer' is associated not with Wyatt, Diamond, or The Monkees, but with an animated ogre. The film *Shrek* (2001), the first in a franchise, introduced a new generation to the song; the film's fairytale wedding finale between Shrek and Princess Fiona features a pumped-up, steroidal version sung by California rock band Smash Mouth, with contributions from Eddie Murphy.

Finally, in 2008, the song came full circle as Neil Diamond recorded a stripped-down acoustic version for his *Dreams* album. His rendition on the BBC's Jools Holland show is exquisite,

Diamond's gravelly delivery ripe with the wisdom of experience. Contestants on TV talent shows these days are often told by the judges (usually Louis Walsh) that they have 'owned' a song. 'You took that song and made it your own,' is the mantra. Diamond, of course, having written the song, already 'owned' it, but here he repossessed it.

David Cheal

WUTHERING HEIGHTS

Some songs feel so distinctive when they arrive that they spend their afterlives being celebrated in peculiar ways. Take Kate Bush's 'Wuthering Heights'. As his TV alter ego Alan Partridge, Steve Coogan sang it at 1999's *Comic Relief*. For the same charity telethon in 2011, Noel Fielding aped Bush's famously theatrical dance moves, and wore a red dress like the one she wore in a promotional video for the single. Then things went crazy: 390 Kate Bushes, similarly clad in flowing scarlet, recreated the video in Brighton's Stanmer Park in 2013. By 2016, The Most Wuthering Heights Day Ever was doing the same in 18 cities, including Sydney, Tel Aviv and Amsterdam.

But however outlandish Bush's debut single seemed, 'Wuthering Heights' was not a song without precedent. Jefferson Airplane's Grace Slick was singing in an upfront, wild style about a nineteenth-century literary classic back in 1967 ('White Rabbit' riffed off Lewis Carroll's *Alice's Adventures in Wonderland*, and became a countercultural classic, as well as a US Top 10 hit). Five years before 'Wuthering Heights', David Bowie was making deeply unusual, piano-led songs for the pop market, and indeed, the young Bush was a fan. 'He was one of my great heroes when I was growing up,' she told *The Fader* magazine in 2016. 'A brave artist, so unusual.'

Bush was incredibly young – signed to EMI at only 16 – and

looked like a 1970s magazine cover star, but she wasn't static and silent. In 'Wuthering Heights', she wails and whoops in a high pitch, her melodies swooping and diving like a bird going in for its prey. Her song's subject matter – Emily Brontë's only novel – was also intellectual, and this teenager talked about it intellectually. 'When I first read *Wuthering Heights* I thought the story was so strong,' Bush told *Record Mirror* in February 1978. 'It was a real challenge to précis the whole mood of a book . . . and this young girl in an era when the female role was so inferior, coming out with this passionate, heavy stuff.'

Bush was captivated by Cathy Earnshaw, Heathcliff's foster sister and great lost love, whose ghost visits the story's narrator, Mr Lockwood, in the novel's third chapter. Bush said that her commitment to the character was helped by the fact that she was born Catherine, not Kate; her family called her Cathy when she was a child. 'I found myself able to relate to her,' she said. 'It's so important to put yourself in the role of the person in a song . . . when I sing that song, I am Cathy.'

Bush's commitment to 'Wuthering Heights' went into her career planning, too. She fought EMI to make it her debut single (they preferred the straighter, poppier 'James and the Cold Gun'). Its release was also postponed from November 1977 because Bush hated the picture they had chosen for its cover. This delay was fortuitous: Wings' 'Mull of Kintyre' had just begun its nine-week reign at Number 1, becoming the first British single to sell more than 2 million copies. 'Wuthering Heights' reached Number 1 on 5 March 1978, becoming the first UK chart-topper to be written and performed by a female artist.

So connected to Bush's image is 'Wuthering Heights' that successful cover versions of the song have been few. Pat Benatar recorded a guitar-heavy cover for her 1980 album *Crimes of*

Passion, while Swedish electronic pop band Röyksopp have included a version in their live sets since 2011. In the same year, Bush's original took on a new life when a slowed-down 36-minute version became an internet viral hit.

Then came the video re-enactments, kicked off by UK performance art group Shambush! at the 2013 Brighton Fringe Festival. Men and women took part, videos circulated online, and similar events were set up all over the world.

Such events across Australia also became fundraisers for domestic violence charities: in Canberra and Melbourne, thousands of dollars were raised for frontline response services. And to think all this joy and generosity came from one distinctive song, written by a teenager singing and dancing to her own formidable tune. We let her in.

Jude Rogers

LET IT GO

In March 2017 a charity running singing workshops at prisons across the UK announced that the most popular song among inmates was 'Let it Go', the big number from Disney's 2013 animated blockbuster, *Frozen*. Despite the superficial incongruity of old lags carolling along to a song more commonly associated with preschoolers dressed as animated princesses, anyone alive to the profound emotional truths of the film would not be surprised to find it resonating with prisoners struggling to own the guilt and shame of the past and yearning to move on.

For the few souls who have still not seen *Frozen*, 'Let it Go' is delivered by the character of Elsa (the blonde one) on the day she is crowned Queen of Arendelle. As a child, little Elsa developed magical powers to create ice and snow, with which she accidentally hurt her sister, Anna. So her parents locked her up in their castle, teaching her to control and conceal her dangerous gift. But an emotional upset at her coronation exposes her 'witchcraft' and turns her subjects against her. She flees Arendelle – the force of her fear and anger leaving eternal winter in her wake – and delivers 'Let it Go' as she strides into the mountains where she finally unleashes her powers to build a dazzling ice palace, create a sexy new outfit and shut herself away from a world she kisses off with a defiant shrug of a line: 'The cold never bothered me anyway.'

Based on the fairy tale of *The Snow Queen*, Elsa was originally written as a villain. But when Broadway songwriters Kristen Anderson-Lopez and Robert Lopez set out to write 'Elsa's Badass Song', the couple realized they were writing 'a transformation song', which Elsa begins as a vulnerable girl and ends as a powerful woman. 'Who doesn't have something there?' says Anderson-Lopez. 'Shame or a secret that keeps them from owning their own power? We dug into that and imagined how it would feel at a much higher level.'

The film was rewritten to suit the song, making Elsa a flawed heroine, saved by the true love of her sister (not the traditional Prince Charming). Melodically, the song circles the sadness of minor chords and blasts exhilaration through the majors. Its unusual structure includes phases of ballad and soft rock with an orchestral centrepiece, ending on a lingering, unresolved chord. Its vocabulary is unpatronizingly advanced, with Elsa's soul 'spiralling in frozen fractals all around / And one thought crystallizes like an icy blast / I'm never going back, the past is in the past!'

That last, long, high exclamation was written for the dynamic vocal range of Broadway powerhouse Idina Menzel, whose in-film version massively outsold Demi Lovato's poppier version (played over the end credits) which Disney had expected to be the big single. It was inevitable that children would connect with the song's bold expression of latent power. But they weren't alone. The internet filled up with tributes and parodies. Frazzled mums converted the chorus to 'F*** it all!' and dads pleaded 'Let it go / I'm gonna smash the radio'. It became a coming out anthem for those expressing LGBT feelings, suffering from mental illness or on the autistic spectrum (like Anderson-Lopez's younger brother).

To bawl along is pure release: the official singalong version has racked up more than 1 billion YouTube views, almost double that of the standard version. It's the most successful Disney song of all time, in the highest grossing animated film (and third highest grossing film) of all time. It's been recorded in over 40 languages and almost every genre, although (with the exception of a patchy live effort by Pearl Jam in 2014) major artists have steered clear, knowing this one's for the fans. Brighton folk rocker Passenger does regularly receive requests for it at gigs, from people muddling it with his 2012 hit, 'Let Her Go'. Anybody interested in how those two songs sound when spliced together should check out the glorious mash-up by YouTuber Sam Tsui. It'll give you shivers.

Helen Brown

HOTEL CALIFORNIA

It started, as things did in the heyday of rock music's golden era, with a few strums of a guitar on a beach sofa in Malibu. Don Felder, guitarist of The Eagles, improvised a chord progression that he recorded on to a cassette, and handed to the rest of the band. The group's de facto leaders, Glenn Frey and Don Henley, liked the song's easy fusion of Hispanic melody and soft reggae beat. Henley started to write a lyric, set in a West Coast hostelry, and addressing the issue of the US's slow implosion into decadence. 'Hotel California' was born. The song was the title track of an album of the same name, released in December 1976, which represented The Eagles' finest hour. They started as a wannabe country rock band with great hair and sumptuous harmonies. After *Hotel California*, they lost their touch.

The release of 'Hotel California' as a single marked a watershed for the band, but also for the course of popular music. Where did it come from? The melody, at least, was familiar. Some pointed out its similarity to a Jethro Tull song, 'We Used to Know', from the British group's 1969 *Stand Up* album. The coincidence was pointed out to Tull's frontman, Ian Anderson, who recalled that the two groups had toured together in the early 1970s, and that there may have been subliminal cross-infection. 'They were countrified, laid-back, polite rock and we were a bit wacky and English and doing weird stuff,' he recounted. But there were no hard feelings. The success of 'Hotel California' gave him a 'sense of happiness'.

The song, clocking in at six-and-a-half minutes, and featuring a coda of dovetailing guitar solos, made an unlikely single. Its ascent to the top of the US charts was slow-moving, as if the pop-buying public was only gradually absorbing the import of its message. Not surprising: the message was obscure, laden with troubling images which belied the melody's appealing simplicity. The song's writers were asked about it, over and over. They responded with references, not entirely unpretentious, to *The Magus* and *The Twilight Zone*. Detractors detected Satanic undertones. Henley finally summed it up briskly: it was a journey, he said, 'from innocence to experience', that skirted 'the fine line between the American dream and the American nightmare'.

'Hotel California' hit the UK Top 10 too. Britain's pop scene was in the throes of the punk revolt, in the midst of which the song's existential doodling seemed irrelevant. But it was a cheerfully eclectic time: sharing the charts with The Eagles in the week of 'Hotel California's' highest, eighth-placed position in April 1977, let's remember, were ABBA, David Soul and Boney M.

The Eagles' tours became grander and longer, and 'Hotel California' became their show-stopper. The song grew more ornate: versions were played with eight guitars, trumpet introductions, a heavier-than-ever sense of portent. Rock music, in its great-haired, sumptuous-harmonied incarnation, was dying. And yet it was making more money than ever. The supergroup at the centre of it all had nailed that sense of paradox: 'This could be heaven and this could be hell'.

There have been few meaningful covers of 'Hotel California'. Techno versions by the likes of Alabama 3 and Jam on the Mutha were ham-fisted attempts to subvert the song's easy-listening charm. The Cat Empire, an Australian band, turned it into a ska anthem, sung in French. The song's accessibility is deceptive: amateur guitarists can pick up the chords easily enough, but accomplished guitarists struggle to match the fluent ferocity of the famous coda.

But it is, in the end, the spirit of 'Hotel California' that survives most potently: its mysterious air of claustrophobia and decline, its Buñuel-ish sense of impotence. The opaque lyrics, today, make more sense than ever: we are way more 'Tiffany-twisted' than we were in 1976. And will there ever be a more perfectly crafted summation of the Brexit blues than that gnomic last line echoing from 40 years ago, 'You can check out any time you like, but you can never leave'?

Peter Aspden

RASPUTIN

Boney M's 1978 single tells a strange and far-reaching story, one that involves a Russian mystic, a German–Caribbean dance group and the explosion of disco behind the Iron Curtain: 'Rasputin' is a dance-floor classic – disco claps and a grooving bassline, embellished by the Slavic twang of a three-stringed balalaika, plus outbreaks of chanting and spoken interludes. Lyrically, it charts a highly speculative biography of Grigory Rasputin: mystic healer, close confidant of the Empress Alexandra and, in Boney M's telling, 'Russia's greatest love machine'.

It's hard to reflect on Boney M's musical output as distinct from the four-piece's flamboyant stage presence. When performing 'Rasputin' live, frontman Bobby Farrell would dance, spin and scissor-kick his way round the stage, sometimes wearing a straggly fake beard – a suitably wild narrator for a song that culminates in the brutal murder of its protagonist.

But Farrell, perhaps the most famous man ever to leave the tiny Caribbean island of Aruba, rarely actually sang unless compelled to do so live. The gravelly male vocals in 'Rasputin' are the work of Frank Farian, the German producer and song-writer who had assembled Boney M in 1975 as a visual front for his songs. No one is quite sure why this early Europop outfit were chosen by Soviet premier Leonid Brezhnev to be the first major Western act to play in the USSR. Perhaps it was because their carnival costumes and singalong melodies put them on the safe side of outré – enough to excite the restless younger generation, but unlikely to incite them to any real rebellion.

It certainly wasn't 'Rasputin' that got Boney M the gig. While it might be imagined that a song about the excesses of Tsarist Russia would have found a ready audience in the Kremlin, it was excluded from their 1978 Red Square concert because of its sexually suggestive lyrics. The ban didn't stop the tune from becoming a hit behind the Iron Curtain. 'Rasputin' quickly became a staple of youth-club dance floors and house band set lists across the Soviet Union. The following year, during a visit to Poland, the group defied the communist authorities and played it live.

'Rasputin' has continued to travel well. Finnish folk-metal band Turisas released their loud, accelerated cover as a single in 2007. In 2012 the noted Indian composer Pritam Chakraborty acquired the rights to remake the song as 'I'll Do the Talking Tonight', an electropop number that appeared as a choreographed dance sequence in the Bollywood spy film *Agent Vinod* the same year. Meanwhile the entrepreneurial Farian turned his back catalogue into a jukebox stage musical. *Daddy Cool*, which premiered at London's Shaftesbury Theatre in 2006 and has toured occasionally in the decade since, tells a familiar story of star-crossed lovers from rival gangs. 'Rasputin' proved one of the harder hits to crowbar into the plot; the 'lover of the Russian queen' became the more prosaic 'hero of the London scene', a DJ and music producer. Thankfully, the wonderfully dated description of Rasputin as 'a cat that really was gone' remained intact.

Boney M were not involved in the musical. The group had

split in 1986 and become embroiled in legal disputes with each other and with Farian. But all four continued to tour their back catalogue separately, and the former Soviet states remained among their most loyal fans. In 2007, the Georgian government invited original member Marcia Barrett to play a gig in war-torn South Ossetia in a bid to convince separatist rebels that life would be better if they didn't leave.

In a curious twist, Bobby Farrell died in his hotel room after playing an energetic concert in St Petersburg on 30 December 2010: on the same date and in the same town as Rasputin had been murdered 94 years previously.

Harriet Fitch Little

6

SEVEN NATION ARMY

'Oh! Je-re-my Coooor-byn!' Forget headliners Radiohead, Foo Fighters and Ed Sheeran: Glastonbury 2017 was all about the Labour Party leader. His name was chanted far beyond the stage where he spoke, at the silent disco and in toilet queues, to the tune of The White Stripes' 'Seven Nation Army'. Online music service Deezer reported a 16,893 per cent spike in streams of the rock band's track, which reached Number 7 in the UK singles chart and a disappointing 76 on the US Billboard Hot 100 when it was first released in 2003.

Classical music buffs may recognize the celebrated seven-note riff from the first movement of Bruckner's Fifth Symphony. But The White Stripes' Jack White came up with it, apparently unaware of the Bruckner work, during a sound check at the Corner Hotel in Melbourne. Sensing a breakthrough in his mission to reinvent the raw blues for modern indie kids, he played it repeatedly for bandmate (and ex-wife) Meg White and their friend Ben Swank. 'I seemed to be the only person who thought it interesting at the time,' White said.

Running his semi-acoustic 1950s Kay Hollowbody guitar through a DigiTech Whammy pitch-shifting pedal, he set it down an octave to create a menacing bass sound to match lyrics about a celebrity confronting the hurt of hometown gossip. As for the title: 'Seven Nation Army' is how White, the seventh son of devout Catholics (who only ruled out the priesthood when he learnt he couldn't take his guitar to the seminary), mispronounced 'Salvation Army' as a child.

Constructed from the Detroit band's signature trio of guitar, vocal and drums, the song was recorded at Toe Rag Studios in Hackney, east London, using only equipment dating from before 1960. That relentless riff runs, unusually, through both the verse and chorus. White fought resistance from his UK and US labels to release it as the first single from The White Stripes' fourth album, *Elephant*.

Although nothing can match the squalling ferocity of the original cut, the song has been covered many times. The Flaming Lips added surreal lyrics in 2005. Kate Nash stropped through it in her estuary accent over a thumped keyboard in 2008. French soul singer Ben l'Oncle Soul gave it a breezy funk-pop makeover in 2010 and his arrangement was borrowed by *X Factor* runner-up Marcus Collins in 2012. Postmodern Jukebox gave it a cheeky smoulder in a 2015 New Orleans jazz version.

But the riff, in isolation, has taken on a life of its own. The *New Yorker* magazine's Alec Wilkinson recently argued that: 'It might be the second-best-known guitar phrase in popular music, after the one from "Satisfaction".' Its migration to the football terraces has been traced back to a European Champions League game in Milan in 2003 between Club Brugge KV of Belgium and AC Milan. The visiting Brugge supporters were in a bar before the game and heard the song over the sound system; they turned Jack White's riff into a wordless chant. After a surprise win against Milan, Brugge adopted the chant as the unofficial club anthem. In 2006, when Brugge lost to AS Roma, the chant was picked up by visiting Italian fans. 'I had never heard the song before we stepped on the field in Bruges,' Roma

captain Francesco Totti told a Dutch newspaper. 'Since then, I can't get the "Po po-po-po po-po" out of my head. It sounded fantastic and the crowd was immediately totally into it. I quickly went out and bought one of the band's albums.'

From there it became the Italian national team's anthem in the 2006 World Cup, with team members joining The Rolling Stones to sing it onstage after their win (the words 'Campione del mondo' were a perfect fit for the riff). It's now rare to attend a major sporting event where the riff isn't played or sung.

It was a short hop from the sporting to the political arena. Egyptian columnist Mona Eltahawy claimed it as the perfect anthem for the youth-backed 2011 uprising against dictator Hosni Mubarak. The riff transferred directly to Corbyn from the soccer pitch when the Labour leader spoke at Prenton Park, home of Tranmere Rovers FC, in May 2017. In a recent interview White said that his entire career has been about 'identifying with the underdog, becoming the over-dog, being punished for that, retreating, advancing, learning to live in modern times'. The Labour leader can surely relate to that.

Helen Brown

HEARTBREAK HOTEL

When the 40th anniversary of Elvis Presley's death was commemorated in 2017, there was inevitably a great deal of morbid interest in the circumstances of the singer's final moments. But there is morbidity, too, in Presley's first Number 1 single, 'Heartbreak Hotel', released in January 1956 and a national breakthrough for the singer following a series of regional hits.

Presley had recorded the song earlier in January for his new label, RCA, and when his old boss at Sun Records, Sam Phillips, heard an acetate of the recording, he declared it a 'morbid mess', while many executives at RCA were similarly unimpressed by its downbeat mood. Yet it stayed at Number 1 in the US for eight weeks, and also inspired countless musicians, among them John Lennon and Keith Richards, for whom hearing this darkly thrilling song was a musical awakening.

The song itself has a murky history. For years the tale was told by its writers, Tommy Durden and Mae Boren Axton, that the lyrics – in particular the line about 'lonely street' – were inspired by a story in the *Miami Herald* of a man who committed suicide and left a note which read, 'I walk a lonely street'. Hours of diligent digging by journalists and researchers failed to yield a relevant article in the *Herald*. Then, in 2016, *Rolling Stone* reckoned it had finally unearthed the true story behind the song. It concerned Alvin Krolik, a career criminal who had found redemption, handing himself in to Chicago police with a confession and a note: 'This is the story of a person who walked a lonely street. I hope this will help someone in the future.' The story caught on among newspapers (though not the *Miami Herald*).

A couple of years later Krolik returned to his criminal ways, robbing a liquor store, where he was shot dead by the owner. The death of the man who 'walked a lonely street' once again hit the headlines, and *Rolling Stone* is convinced that this was the story that inspired Durden and Axton. Whatever: when Presley was first played a demo of the song by Axton in a hotel room, he is reported to have said, 'Hot dog, Mae, play that again!'

'Heartbreak Hotel' is an eight-bar blues, taken at quite a lick by Presley and his studio band, which included the great guitarist Chet Atkins. It was Presley's idea to use a hallway in the studio to create the song's distinctive echo. Presley was given a one-third writing credit, essentially as a sweetener for agreeing to record the song. Over the years Presley continued to play it; a TV comeback special in 1968 shows him on knock-about form, laughing and forgetting the lyrics. He last sang it on 29 May 1977 at the Civic Center in Baltimore.

Meanwhile, others – more than 200, at the last count – have tackled the song. Johnny Cash sang a comic, exaggeratedly hip-swivelling version on TV in 1959, which he described as 'an impersonation of a rock'n'roll singer impersonating Elvis'. English folkie Bert Jansch accentuated the bluesiness in his 1982 version. Punk-rockabilly band The Cramps played a typically turbulent version in 1987.

But the version that stands miles above all others came from former Velvet Underground member John Cale. In 1974 Cale was signed to Island Records, whose A&R man Richard Williams planned a promotional concert featuring some of the label's artists. So Cale, Kevin Ayers, Eno and Nico played a show at London's Rainbow Theatre (recorded for an album, *June 1, 1974*). Cale's contribution was a pitch-black, deconstructed version of 'Heartbreak Hotel', driven by a metallic riff and with a vocal melody that bore only a passing resemblance to Presley's. A wailing female backing vocalist added to the horror. Cale later told The Creative Independent website: 'If it didn't have words like that, that song wouldn't have survived. All the verses were really something special . . . It sounded to me like each contributor to the song had gotten a verse in, because if you read the verses, they're about very different things. They make a very rich portrait of a character.'

Cale reprised the song for his 1975 *Slow Dazzle* album and has continued to revisit it in live shows over the years; it has been acclaimed by some music critics as the finest cover version of all time. Growling, howling and grinding, it mines the song's darkness, and takes 'morbid' to a whole new level.

David Cheal

GEORGIA ON MY MIND

The languid, almost sensuous lyrics of 'Georgia on My Mind' could as easily be about a lover as the southern US state the 1930 song celebrates. Certainly, the line 'Other arms reach out to me, other eyes smile tenderly' suggests that a woman (or man) might be involved. But combine Stuart Gorrell's lyrics with Hoagy Carmichael's music and the sense of place becomes palpable.

Yet Indiana-raised Carmichael had never set foot in Georgia when he composed the tune. What's more, it seems that the idea for the song wasn't even his. According to his biographer, Richard M Sudhalter, it was the saxophonist Frank Trumbauer who suggested Georgia as a subject. After all, he reasoned: 'Nobody ever lost money writing songs about the South.'

Carmichael recorded the song in September 1930. This 'Georgia' mixes sentiment and hot jazz, features Carmichael's vocals and, towards the end, a short eight-bar break from his friend Bix Beiderbecke. It is the cornetist/trumpeter's last-known session: Biederbecke, an alcoholic, died the following year at the age of 28.

But it was the originator of the idea for the song, Trumbauer, who had the first hit with it. His equally jazzy version made the US Top 10 in 1931, as did Mildred Bailey's recording that same year. Although many versions followed, hits proved elusive. The drummer Gene Krupa and his orchestra reached Number 17 in 1941 with Anita O'Day on vocals but the rock'n'roll 1950s were a barren period for both the song and its composer. Carmichael, who ended up acting and writing music for the TV western series Laramie, once told *Downbeat* magazine: 'After rock and roll started, I never even got a phone call from an A&R [artists and repertoire] man about anything.'

But in 1960 the song's fortunes changed. Rising star Ray Charles had left Atlantic Records in order to gain greater artistic control, higher royalties and mainstream acceptance at a time when albums were starting to outsell singles. His first LP for his new label ABC-Paramount was *The Genius Hits the Road*, a 12-track concept album themed on places in the US; 'Georgia on My Mind', the standout track, was sandwiched between 'Alabamy Bound' and 'Basin Street Blues'. Released as a single, it reached Number 1 in November 1960 and won a Grammy Award. Charles's performance wrung every ounce out of the song's yearning-for-home theme; his live renditions were even more moving. Yet according to his 1978 autobiography, *Brother Ray*, neither woman nor state were on his mind when he recorded the song. 'I've never known a lady named Georgia . . . and I wasn't dreaming of the state . . . even though I was born there,' he said. 'It was just a beautiful, romantic melody.'

That didn't stop 'Georgia on My Mind' becoming so indelibly linked to the southern state that in 1979 the relationship was formalized when the Georgia House of Representatives declared it the official state song.

Charles's 1960 hit ushered in a plethora of covers, including The Band's 1976 endorsement single for presidential hopeful Jimmy Carter. But it was Willie Nelson who had a substantial hit with it when he topped Billboard's country and western

chart in 1978 and won the song a second Grammy. In 2005 the Albany rap group Field Mob's 'Georgia', with Atlanta-raised Ludacris and Jamie Foxx (who played Ray Charles in the 2004 biopic), bookended a rap on the gritty reality of the state's underbelly with the rose-tinted yearnings of Carmichael and Gorrell's song. The idea worked, not least because 'Georgia on My Mind' is a brilliant work of imaginative fiction that captures the yearnings of the homesick soul. That fact and fantasy are so out of step only adds to the pathos.

Mike Hobart

WATERLOO SUNSET

Puzzles and contradictions surround 'Waterloo Sunset', its composer and the city in which it is set. It is the quintessential London song – yet Ray Davies originally called it 'Liverpool Sunset'. The song lauded by The Who's Pete Townshend as 'divine' and 'a masterpiece' soundtracked the swinging '60s, but its composer had in mind the aspirations of an earlier generation. And although its lyric appears to be a narrative, 'Waterloo Sunset' is as dappled and impressionistic as the Summer of Love that it heralded.

The original idea for The Kinks' 1967 hit came to Davies in a dream. He wrote an early iteration in tribute to Liverpool: he adored the city's Merseybeat sound and wanted to acknowledge The Kinks' popularity in the city. But he relocated it after concluding that it was better to work with what you know.

Davies certainly knew Waterloo. In 1951, his parents had taken him to that celebration of all things British, the Festival of Britain, located on the South Bank around Waterloo; as a patient just down the Thames at St Thomas' Hospital aged 13, he had gazed from a balcony at the Houses of Parliament; he had travelled from Waterloo Station as a Croydon School of Art student; he had wooed his first wife, Rasa Didzpetris, on Waterloo Bridge.

'It keeps popping up in my life,' he says. 'The images got

into my psyche.' The 'dirty old river' of the opening line is 'like the artery of the city, where the blood flows, pumps through the city and gives it life'.

But who were Terry and Julie, the characters in 'Waterloo Sunset' who meet every Friday night? Many have assumed that Davies had in mind Terence Stamp and Julie Christie, who were famous at the time for co-starring in the film *Far From the Madding Crowd*. In fact he was thinking of one of his older sister's tales of her wartime childhood. In the song Davies imagines her and her boyfriend going across to a better life north of the river.

Davies played the song to the rest of The Kinks at his semi-detached suburban house in Fortis Green, north London – although he felt protective enough over the lyrics to prevent his bandmates from hearing them until the recording, at Pye Records' basement studio in Marble Arch.

The backing track was simple: Davies played acoustic guitar with bassist Pete Quaife and drummer Mick Avory, then over-dubbed a piano at the coda along with his brother Dave's distinctive guitar part, which was innovatively recorded with tape echo. The harmonies, sung by Rasa, Dave Davies and Quaife, added a dreamlike aspect to the recording.

The song has been covered many times, but none has been able to match the perfection of The Kinks' sublime original. The Jam, who had had a minor hit with The Kinks' 'David Watts', made a ham-fisted stab at it in 1980, but wisely left it unreleased for 30 years. David Bowie had recorded The Kinks' 'Where Have all the Good Times Gone?' for his 1973 covers album, *Pin Ups*, and covered 'Waterloo Sunset' in a similar style, as a bonus track to some editions of his *Reality* album in 2003; that same year, he also sang it with Davies at a charity concert.

Def Leppard turned in a surprisingly faithful rendition for a 2006 covers album, doubling down on Dave Davies's crunchy guitar sound. By contrast, Peter Gabriel's orchestral take in 2010 departs from The Kinks' arrangement – while managing to make it sound somehow even more English.

Davies himself has re-recorded it, as an autumnal acoustic duet with Jackson Browne for his 2010 album *See My Friends*. He has also written a book of short stories entitled *Waterloo Sunset* and a film called *Return to Waterloo*. The location remains significant.

'If there's anyone in my life who's important,' he says, 'I like to take them to Waterloo Bridge, to stand on the bridge with them to see if it feels good.'

Jon Dennis

ODE TO BILLIE JOE

Money, Mississippi, has a population of about 100. The settlement is famous for two things. One is real: in 1955, a 14-year-old boy, Emmett Till, was lynched, a murder referred to in songs by The Staple Singers and Bob Dylan. The other is fictional: Bobbie Gentry's 'Ode to Billie Joe'.

An atmospheric production that mixed country music with funky R&B, 'Ode to Billie Joe' is an enigma. Its storyline is clear enough; some of the details are not. Billie Joe McAllister has jumped off the Tallahatchie Bridge in Money into the river below and, over dinner, a family offer opinions about their deceased acquaintance. Gentry sings of apple pie, cutting cotton, a prank involving frogs and, eventually, the death of the family's father from a virus.

Gradually the closeness of the song's narrator to Billie Joe becomes apparent; she and Billie had been seen throwing something off the bridge on the day before he leapt to his death. Exactly what, is left to the listener's imagination. At the end of the song, the narrator whiles away time throwing something else from the bridge: flowers, a lament to Billie Joe, her lost, unspoken love.

'Ode to Billie Joe' had started as an eight-minute acoustic epic, scheduled as the B-side of Gentry's debut single before Capitol Records realized its potential. The song had almost half

its length excised, and Jimmie Haskell's edgy, swooping strings did nothing to impinge on the understated atmosphere of Gentry's song. Its juxtaposition of banalities against profound loss struck a chord in the US of 1967, which was keeping up appearances while fighting in Vietnam, watching its leaders being assassinated, and coping with change wrought by the civil rights movement. It was the US's third biggest-selling single of the year. Gentry was repeatedly asked what had been thrown from the bridge – a ring, a baby? She shrugged: 'Everybody has a different guess.'

Gentry's song triggered copycat leaps from the Tallahatchie Bridge. The wooden structure was 6 metres high, so the fall was unlikely to kill unless the river was in flood. The authorities, tired of sorting out the mess, introduced a bylaw that fined jumpers $100.

The haunting feel of 'Ode to Billie Joe' attracted sax players. Lou Donaldson and Willis Jackson both covered it, losing out to King Curtis, who scored a Top 30 US hit with a wailing cover, just months after the original was issued. Tommy McCook, a Jamaican saxophonist, gave Curtis's template a gentle rocksteady-styled makeover in 1968.

Singers also offered tributes to Billie Joe. Gentry was ahead of the 'rebel-country' movement and fellow insurgent Lee Hazlewood was an early adopter of her song in 1967. Motown trio The Supremes cooed it; southern soul star Joe Tex, who loved to talk through story songs, was cut out for it. One of the most interesting interpretations was by Joe Dassin, a French vocalist who retitled it 'Marie-Jeanne', reversing the sexes and setting it amid vineyards rather than cotton fields. Bob Dylan wrote a parody, 'Clothes Line Saga', and Roger White (actually country star Johnny Paycheck) offered 'Mystery of Tallahatchie

Bridge', which attempted to fill perceived gaps. In 1976, a film, *Ode to Billy Joe*, had the titular character making his jump after a gay sexual experience. Perhaps this Hollywood cliché was too much for the poor fella.

Bobbie Gentry showed no interest in filling in her song's details. She said it was about 'the basic indifference, the casualness of people in moments of tragedy'. Perhaps tired of being associated with one composition, the talented composer retired in 1981 at the age of 37 and has not appeared in public since. As if unable to bear the weight of its cultural significance, the original Tallahatchie Bridge at Money collapsed in 1972, after it was set alight by vandals.

Ian McCann

GIMME! GIMME! GIMME! (A MAN AFTER MIDNIGHT)

In 1971, Sweden became the second country in the world after Denmark to decriminalize pornography. That year Agnetha Fältskog married Björn Ulvaeus. They were in a cabaret act with another romantically involved duo, Benny Andersson and Anni-Frid Lyngstad. It was called Festfolket.

The name was a pun on the Swedish words for 'party people' and 'engaged couples'. The following year the foursome became ABBA. Trading on their status as couples, their image was as clean as their dazzling smiles.

Yet they were not untouched by Sweden's reputation for sexual permissiveness.

The blonde Fältskog was an unwilling sex symbol; her response to a 1977 review in an Australian newspaper lauding 'Agnetha's bottom' as 'a Swedish national treasure' was to groan: 'Oh my God! Don't they have bottoms in Australia?'

But ABBA were not above feeding those fantasies, too. The theme of sexual liberation runs through their music, from the 17-year-old 'teaser' in 'Dancing Queen' to the absurd schoolroom seduction in 'When I Kissed the Teacher'. A journalist visiting Andersson's office in 1976 noted a life-size painting of a scantily dressed young woman, 'the only sign of decadence in the whole ABBA operation'.

'Gimme! Gimme! Gimme! (A Man After Midnight)' is a

masterpiece of Scandinavian frankness. It was recorded in August 1979 for a North American tour. Sung by Fältskog, it is about a depressed woman alone in a flat watching late-night television as an autumn wind howls outside. 'Gimme, gimme, gimme a man after midnight,' she cries. 'Won't somebody help me chase the shadows away?'

Her gothic tale of alienation and sexual frustration unfolds to the pulse of a libidinous disco beat: the disco craze was at its peak in 1979. The song's video, made by Swedish film director Lasse Hallström, shows it being recorded in the state-of-the-art Polar Studios in Stockholm, which ABBA had built. The headphones that Fältskog is filmed wearing were among the exhibits at the ABBA-themed *ABBA: Super Troupers* which was on show in 2018 at London's Southbank Centre.

The video opens with a close-up shot of a pair of hands pushing sliders on a mixing desk, a sign of the group's adaptation to new pop technologies. Hallström had used a similar opening shot several years earlier in his video for ABBA's 1973 single 'Ring Ring', although back then the hands were playing a jaunty tune on an old-fashioned piano.

The quartet had come a long way as musicians, and as individuals. At the start of 1979 Fältskog and Ulvaeus filed for divorce; Lyngstad and Andersson separated the following year. In 'Gimme! Gimme! Gimme!', Fältskog found herself in the awkward position of singing verses about a woman's desperate urge for sex that had been written by her lyricist ex-husband, who by that point had rebounded into the arms of a new girl-friend. The dazzling smile must have ached.

Yet the song has a feminist aspect too. Sung with disco-diva power by Fältskog, with Lyngstad on backing vocals, it gives unambiguous voice to female desire. Perhaps fearing that it

might prove too bracing for less sexually egalitarian cultures, 'man' was swapped for 'love' when they recorded a Spanish version, 'Dame! Dame! Dame! (Amor Esta Noche)'.

After ABBA ended in 1982 their music became a byword for cheesy pop. But 'Gimme! Gimme! Gimme!' lived on as a gay anthem. In 1986 the synth-pop duo Erasure paid tribute to it with a hi-NRG cover version, the B-side to their single 'Oh L'Amour'. The song featured on 1992's *Gold: Greatest Hits*, which restored the band's commercial fortunes with 30 million sales. It was also reactivated by pop's queen of sexual liberation, Madonna. Her 2005 hit single 'Hung Up' was based on a sample of the irresistible synthesizer riff that runs through 'Gimme! Gimme! Gimme!'. It was only the second time that ABBA had licensed their music as a sample (The Fugees used 'The Name of the Game' in their 1996 song 'Rumble in the Jungle'). Madonna said she wrote to them 'begging' to be allowed to use it. Andersson, who composed ABBA's music, framed the letter. Perhaps it hangs in place of the louche painting of the young woman.

Ludovic Hunter-Tilney

12

GREENSLEEVES

Tinkling across the tarmac on summer afternoons, 'Greensleeves' has been luring British children to ice cream vans since 1958. The olde folk song in its melancholy minor key was an odd choice of jingle for the UK's first fleet of Mr Whippy ice cream vans. But the company's British-born founder, Dominic Facchino, turns out to have been a big fan of Henry VIII, so topped his Mr Whippy character with a floppy Tudor hat and supplied his vendors with wind-up music boxes of a song widely believed to have been written by Henry for his second wife, Anne Boleyn.

Alas, although Henry VIII was a gifted musician, it is unlikely that the king (who died in 1547) wrote a song whose lyrics were first registered by London printer Richard Jones as 'A new Northern Dittye of the Lady Greene Sleeves' in 1580. It's possible that the melody has changed over time, but the version we know today is written in the Spanish romanesca style which didn't reach England until after Henry's death. The tune rises and falls with the hopes of a lover 'discourteously' rejected by a woman he has wooed with gifts including a 'petticoat of slender white / With gold embroidered gorgeously'.

There's a theory that the object of the singer's affection is either promiscuous or a prostitute: her sleeves would be green from rolling in the grass. But in songs of the time green was also symbolic of growing love or unmarried young women.

Whatever the meaning, the song was clearly well known by the time Shakespeare wrote *The Merry Wives of Windsor* in 1597 – in that play Falstaff exclaims: 'Let the sky rain potatoes! Let it thunder to the tune of "Greensleeves"!' – and remains in the mainstream more than 400 years later.

Its 18-note melody was drafted as a military march by the Cavaliers in the English Civil War and the homesick Tommies in the First World War. Its innate Englishness appealed to Ralph Vaughan Williams, who worked it into the third act of his 1928 Shakespeare-inspired opera *Sir John in Love*, rearranged in 1934 by Ralph Greaves as the popular classic 'Fantasia on Greensleeves'.

Perhaps it was the tune's sheer age and cosy nostalgia value that eventually saw it hitched to Christmas. In 1865 it was refitted as the Christmas carol, 'What Child Is This?', with lyrics by Bristol poet William Chatterton Dix. In this form it has been served – sweet'n'gloopy as eggnog – by a holy host of sentimental crooners: Johnny Mathis (1958), Andy Williams (1974) and Glen Campbell (1993). In 1968 Frank Sinatra kept the festive theme but opted for more secular lyrics when singing it with kids Nancy, Tina and Frank Jnr as 'The Bells of Christmas' in 1968. The carol has had edgier treatment in the noughties, attracting the attention of alternative singer–songwriters like Sufjan Stevens (2002), Tori Amos (2012) and The Red House Painters' Mark Kozelek (2014), whose thoughtful growl rescues it from nylon-stringed tweeness.

The folk revival which peaked in the 1960s found many earnest troubadours harking back to the antique language of the original, but more audacious performers added a modern rock twist. Marianne Faithfull added tense strings and drums on the B-side of her 1964 hit, 'As Tears Go By'. Leonard Cohen sexed up the lyrics on 1974's 'Leaving Green Sleeves'.

Hollywood picked up on the revived hipness of 'Greensleeves' and recast it as 'A Home in the Meadow' in the 1962 MGM epic, *How the West Was Won*, in which Debbie Reynolds' winsome delivery prompts a proposal from Gregory Peck. Elvis swaggered it out as 'Stay Away' for his 1968 comedy-western *Stay Away, Joe*.

Jazz has treated it with more class. Oscar Peterson gave it some surprisingly urban sophistication in 1970 but John Coltrane's 1961 version is the standout as his soprano sax sketches depth, confusion and mystery around the familiar theme.

Alas, the circular simplicity that ensures the longevity of 'Greensleeves' also makes it one of the world's most maddening earworms. A poll commissioned by 'Stressbusting' wesbite saw it voted the most annoying song played to callers on hold. 'When "Greensleeves" comes on the line, yet again,' said co-editor Peter Freedman, 'I feel like smashing the phone with a pickaxe.'

Helen Brown

13

JEALOUS GUY

'All the cigarette lighters came out,' said Bryan Ferry about the first time Roxy Music performed John Lennon's 'Jealous Guy'. 'It was a very emotional evening.'

Roxy Music performed the song as an encore during a concert in Germany after Lennon's murder in December 1980. They recorded it the following week, and when it was released as a single in February 1981 it gave them their only UK Number 1. While Lennon's 'Jealous Guy' is confessional and raw, Ferry maintains an elegant emotional detachment. Both versions feature whistling, a confirmation of loneliness and isolation rather than jauntiness.

Lennon wrote the melancholy melody of 'Jealous Guy' for an earlier song called 'Child of Nature'. In February 1968, The Beatles – with wives and girlfriends, roadies, Mia Farrow, Donovan and The Beach Boys' Mike Love in tow – had retreated to Rishikesh, in the foothills of the Himalayas, to learn about transcendental meditation at the ashram of the Maharishi Mahesh Yogi. Lennon, Paul McCartney and George Harrison wrote more than 30 songs there. Even Ringo Starr wrote one.

The Maharishi's lecture on the 'son of mother nature' inspired Lennon to write 'Child of Nature' and McCartney to write its companion piece, 'Mother Nature's Son'. Both songs echo 'Nature Boy', eden ahbez's standard first recorded by Nat King Cole in

1948 (see Chapter 40). Eighteen songs written in Rishikesh made it on to The Beatles' *White Album*, but 'Child of Nature' remains unreleased. The lyrics of 'Child of Nature' touch on some of Lennon's favourite themes: dreaming, freedom and the mother-and-son relationship.

But three years later Lennon rewrote the song, keeping only the words 'I was dreaming' from his earlier composition. Both songs express a rejection of machismo – but while 'Child of Nature' is free of ego, the guilt-ridden narrator of 'Jealous Guy' is only too aware of his. The songs have 'an almost diametrically different outlook', writes Ian MacDonald in his book *Revolution in the Head*.

Lennon admitted that he had been consumed by jealousy, and had even been violent towards women – 'That's why I am always on about peace,' he told *Playboy* magazine. He had alluded to this tendency in The Beatles' songs 'Run for Your Life' and 'Getting Better'. 'Jealous Guy' would appear to be in this lineage, and refer to his relationship with Yoko Ono. However, McCartney told *Playgirl* magazine in 1985: 'He [Lennon] wrote "I'm Just a Jealous Guy", and he said that the song was about me.'

When 'Jealous Guy' was recorded in 1971, the ex-Beatles were speaking to each other via their lawyers and through messages on their solo records. Alongside 'Jealous Guy' on Lennon's *Imagine* album was 'How Do You Sleep?', a vicious attack on his estranged musical partner – abetted by Harrison, who played slide guitar on the track. The album also carried a postcard insert featuring Lennon holding a pig in the same pose McCartney had struck with a sheep on the sleeve of his recent album *Ram*.

Whatever its meaning, Lennon liked his song of repentance.

According to his publicist Elliot Mintz, in 1977 Lennon performed the song on acoustic guitar to bemused fellow guests in a Tokyo hotel. It was one of the last times any members of the public saw Lennon play a song.

Soul singer Donny Hathaway's version on his great 1972 live album manages to reach the depths of sadness while sounding surprisingly positive. It is Hathaway's arrangement, with its heavy beat and bar-room piano, that Rod Stewart and the Faces covered to close their 1973 live album. Hathaway's version is also the basis for recordings by Joe Cocker and José Feliciano. Youssou N'Dour and The Deftones also recorded it for a 2007 Amnesty album for Darfur.

But 'Jealous Guy' was a perfect fit for Ferry's persona of the world-weary roué and for Roxy Music's adult rock, which they had by that stage in their career buffed to an icy, immaculate sheen. Their 1981 cover remains definitive.

Jon Dennis

14

I PUT A SPELL ON YOU

Songs can be mixed blessings. Jay Hawkins was a fine singer with an unusual, dated-sounding baritone voice, a talented song-writer, an able pianist and a useful saxophonist. Though he was influenced by Paul Robeson, Hawkins sang the blues. Blues wailers were a dime a dozen in the US of the early 1950s, and he needed a gimmick. He tried looking exotic, wearing leopard-skin suits, a turban and leather. He tried writing tunes about drinking, and women who used curses to find a fella.

The latter two ideas came together when he recorded 'I Put a Spell on You' during a drunken studio session in 1956. The song was to change his life – for both good and ill. While Hawkins imagined his song as a sophisticated ballad, what emerged that day was a wild horror howl, certain to be shelved. But Okeh, his record label, liked it. This staggering funeral march of a ditty, pushed along by a plaintive plunking banjo, was the gimmick he needed. Okeh renamed him Screamin' Jay Hawkins and the horror rock genre was born.

Alan Freed, an early rock'n'roll DJ and promoter, dared Hawkins to appear at his shows in a coffin, dressed as a voodoo priest. Hawkins refused, saying: 'No black dude gets in a coffin alive – they don't expect to get out!' When Freed added a $300 incentive to the proposition, Hawkins changed his mind, later claiming it was $2,000. From this point on, he became a full-time horror-rock performer and his style was appropriated by Screaming Lord Sutch, Kiss and Alice Cooper, among others.

But for Hawkins, there was a price to pay: gone was the sophisticated balladeer he wanted to be. 'I Put a Spell on You' became both a way to earn a living – and a cross to bear. The record sold 1 million copies but it was a cult curiosity, too weird to hit the charts. However, Hawkins proved correct: it worked just as well as a straight, desperate love plea. Nina Simone edited all the gags out of it in a mesmerizing 1965 version. 'I Put a Spell on You' gave Alan Price his first hit in 1966 after leaving The Animals a year earlier, and it helped establish Creedence Clearwater Revival's chart credentials in 1968. None hammed it up: the song stood on its own passionate merits. On the other skeletal, claw-like hand, Arthur Brown returned it to its creepy roots in 1968, adding new lyrics to make it even more melodramatic.

'I Put a Spell on You' brought bliss to all who touched it – except its composer. In 1973, he moaned, 'If it were up to me, I wouldn't be Screamin' Jay Hawkins . . . James Brown did an awful lot of screamin', but never got called Screamin' James Brown . . . Why can't people take me as a regular singer without making a bogeyman out of me?'

By this time, Alice Cooper had become a major rock star with a show that owed plenty to Hawkins' act. *The Rocky Horror Show* spooked theatres, and the sub-genre peaked with Michael Jackson's 'Thriller' in 1983, its video packed with funky zombies. Hawkins was rediscovered as a cult figure during the 1980s, acclaimed for a role in Jim Jarmusch's film *Mystery Train*. He performed his voodoo shtick, armed with skulls, fireworks and sticks, across the US.

'I Put a Spell on You' continued to work its magic. Marilyn

Manson's 1995 cover was all mock-horror. Bryan Ferry and Annie Lennox played it straight, as did Jeff Beck and Joss Stone, whose 2010 version was nominated for a Grammy award. The song has been covered by more than 80 artists. In 2001, a year after Hawkins died, a documentary about his life was released, *I Put a Spell on Me*. It told of his thwarted dream to sing opera. But he was reconciled to his famous song: for Hawkins, its spell had been broken.

Ian McCann

15

MISIRLOU

In 1927, an Istanbul-born Greek musician, Tetos Demetriades, having recently translocated to the US, recorded a piece of music he remembered from his youth. 'Misirlou', loosely translated as 'Egyptian Girl', was a swaying, erotic folk song performed in the rebetiko style that was popular among Greek Anatolians: 'The sweet way you look at me lights flames in my heart . . . honey seeps from your lips.'

The mesmerizing and catchy melody, not credited with a composer, proved popular and the song was performed in a variety of styles in subsequent years. Another Greek, Nikos Roubanis, gave it an instrumental jazz arrangement in 1941, and 'Misirlou' became something of a standard, its sexy 'otherness' adorning many a repertoire of the lounge bands of the time.

It also became something of what we would today call a 'world music sensation': versions were recorded in Arabic and Yiddish, and various communities of the eastern Mediterranean laid claim to the original melody. It continued to ping its way across the globe until it settled in the heart and mind of a young American by the name of Richard Monsour, who was in the process of adopting the racier moniker of Dick Dale.

Dale was of Lebanese descent from his father's side. He had learned the ukulele as a young boy, graduating to the guitar, but fell in love with the more adrenaline-charged pastime of surfing when his family moved to California in 1954. All the elements of a cultish big bang were in place when he was allegedly asked, at one of his concerts, if he could play an entire song on one string of his guitar. Dale remembered 'Misirlou' from his childhood and zapped it out in show-off, double-quick time. The crowd loved it. It was the beginning of the 'surfers' stomp' movement, recalled Dale many years later. Into the studio he went, and 'Misirlou Twist' appeared on his first album, 1962's *Surfers' Choice*. He played it on *The Ed Sullivan Show*.

The Beach Boys heard it, loved it, and recorded it too, on their second album *Surfin' U.S.A.* Within a couple of generations, the heady Anatolian love song had somehow become a frantic anthem for mastering the swells of the Californian waves. Could anything be more postmodern?

Well, yes. In the 1990s, 'Misirlou' came under the irony-loving gaze of Quentin Tarantino, who was putting together the music for his long-awaited follow-up to *Reservoir Dogs*, a pastiche film noir he would call *Pulp Fiction*. The cast included the rising star Uma Thurman and the forgotten star John Travolta. The music used in the film's opening credits was Dick Dale's 'Misirlou'. *Pulp Fiction* was a sensation, audiences falling in love again with Dale's artful stomp. The song that was originally a molten celebration of flaming desire became an exercise in ironic detachment. It subsequently became a signifier of naive 1960s culture, used in such style-conscious works as *Mad Men* (when Don Draper tries to let go of his inhibitions on a trip to LA), and sampled by the Black Eyed Peas in 'Pump It'. The video for that single was a perfect mash-up of pop culture references, in which group leader will.i.am 'fought' with oriental hoodlums in a car park, showed off his (digitally doctored) football skills and generally rapped his way around the old eastern melody with aplomb.

'Misirlou' returned to something of its former glory when it was sung by Greek singer Anna Vissi in the closing ceremony of the Athens 2004 Olympics. How weird it was that the ceremony should include the theme from *Pulp Fiction*, the millions of television spectators must have wondered. Those in the know simply welcomed the old tune, and its lusty homage to a young girl's honeyed lips, back to its homeland.

Peter Aspden

16

A HARD RAIN'S A-GONNA FALL

Dylanologists have endlessly picked over the bones of its genesis, its meaning and its lyrical symbolism. But what we do know about 'A Hard Rain's A-Gonna Fall' is that it was written in 1962 in a room above Greenwich Village's Gaslight Café on a typewriter belonging to the Beat poet and activist later known as Wavy Gravy, and that it went on to become one of the defining songs of the 1960s: a howl of abhorrence in the face of . . . well, pretty much everything: war, obviously, but also poverty, ignorance, want.

Bob Dylan wrote 'Hard Rain' in the style of a centuries-old Scottish border ballad called 'Lord Randal' with its question-and-answer format: 'Oh where have you been, Lord Randal, my son; And where have you been my handsome young man.' (Dylan's melody is similar to 'Lord Randal', too, as is his use of 3/4 time.) But instead of a medieval story of love, betrayal and poisoning, Dylan's 'darling young one' takes up the baton of the Beat poets, relating, in a seven-minute pile-up of chilling images, an apocalyptic vision of bleeding hammers and black branches that drip blood.

He first sang it soon after writing it, downstairs at the Gaslight Café; a bootleg recording, made official in 2005, shows almost no changes to the lyrics between that performance and the studio recording for his *Freewheelin' Bob Dylan* album, except that the former included the line, 'I heard the sound of one person who cried, he was human.'

'Hard Rain' was written, say the album's sleeve notes, 'during the Cuban missile crisis of October 1962'. But in fact the song had been completed several weeks before the crisis. The 'pellets of poison' and the 'hard rain' of the lyrics were not, as many surmised, direct references to nuclear fallout; the poison pellets were the lies told by newspapers, Dylan later said, while the 'hard rain' itself was a more general foreboding of terrible events. Bad stuff, Dylan was saying, is going to happen.

Roll on nine years, and Dylan was now a shadowy figure who hadn't been seen on stage for two years. But then, at 1971's Concert for Bangladesh at New York's Madison Square Garden, this pioneering benefit show's organizer George Harrison made a casual announcement from the stage: 'Like to bring on a friend of us all – Mr Bob Dylan.' Cue audience eruption. Dylan's first song was apposite, given the cause that the concert was supporting: a brisk, up-tempo 'Hard Rain', accompanied by his own guitar, a plunking bass, and decorated by Harrison's gentle bottleneck guitar. Dylan was back in the spotlight.

His song, meanwhile, had taken on a life of its own. Joan Baez recorded the first of several versions on her 1965 album *Farewell, Angelina*, acoustic and electric guitar dovetailing to form a sweet backdrop for her stunning voice. Pianist and singer Leon Russell recorded the first of several stomping versions in 1971. One of the boldest came from Bryan Ferry, who opened his debut solo album *These Foolish Things* (1973) with his unique take on 'Hard Rain', reinvented as a spine-tingling three-minute rock song with jabbing, staccato piano and violin, backing vocals, sound effects (thunder; laughter) and Ferry's dramatic vocal delivery. It's a masterpiece.

Dylan himself has continued to sing 'Hard Rain' over the years, these days in a full-band arrangement in which Dylan, as is now his custom, ignores the actual tune. Live footage on YouTube is followed by comments which generally fall into one of two categories – Dylan is God, or, simply: 'Bob, please stop.'

So it was perhaps wise of Dylan not to appear in person for 2016's Nobel Prize ceremony in Stockholm. Serendipity intervened. Patti Smith had already been chosen to perform at the ceremony before Dylan's literature prize was announced. When Dylan's prize was revealed, she decided to sing 'Hard Rain'. Her version will bring tears to the driest of eyes – despite (well, actually: because of) her stumbling over the lyrics and apologizing. Once she had overcome her nerves, Smith rode the song confidently, her voice crackling with emotion; tears welled up in the white-tied audience of royals and dignitaries. The orchestra added weight and dignity. Bad stuff, Dylan was telling us, is still happening.

David Cheal

17

NIGHT TRAIN

The 1962–63 world heavyweight boxing champion Sonny Liston often trained to the sound of saxophonist Jimmy Forrest's 'Night Train', a huge rhythm and blues hit in 1952. But for the most part the instrumental blues is more bump-and-grind than jab-and-hook. It chugs along at a tempo just up from a smooch, and Forrest's already raw sax is distorted with echo.

Forrest conceived his three-verse blues during a stint with The Duke Ellington Orchestra. The first verse's riff is a roughed-up reading of the elegant 1940 recording by Johnny Hodges, 'That's the Blues, Old Man'. But the second verse borrows heavily from 'Happy Go Lucky Local', the fourth movement of Ellington's *Deep South Suite*, recorded in 1946. Only the stop-time break that opens the third verse was entirely of Forrest's invention.

After the song spent 20 weeks in the charts, cover versions came thick and fast. Saxophonist Earl Bostic added a train whistle and better sound; the Buddy Morrow Orchestra scored a minor 1952 big band hit featuring the leader's trombone. In 1957, jump-and-jive bandleader Louis Prima widened the song's appeal with a televised comedy routine featuring stony-faced singer Keely Smith and wailing saxophonist Sam Butera. In 1960 guitar band The Ventures gave it a country-and-western tinge.

Then James Brown got hold of the song. Brown recorded

'Night Train' in 1961 – while his drummer took a bathroom break during a studio session. Brown told Gerri Hershey, author of *Nowhere to Run: The Story of Soul Music*: 'When he come [sic] back, I had created a million seller playin' the drums myself.' Brown's cover, released in 1962, beefs up the bass with guitar, sits the melody on the choppy rhythms of a boogaloo and moves the tempo up a notch. The track opens with Brown half-shouting 'All aboard the night train' and calling out a list of nationwide destinations.

Brown's reinvention of 'Night Train' was an R&B smash, and crossed over to the pop charts. He liked to use the song as a show-closer, but he never deployed it more devastatingly than in the early pop concert film *The TAMI Show*. Brown was furious that The Rolling Stones – to him mere imitators of R&B – topped the bill over him. Brown chose 'Night Train' to end a legendary, whirlwind four-number performance. In his 1987 autobiography *The Godfather of Soul*, Brown wrote: 'I don't think I'd ever danced so hard in my life, and I don't think [the audience] had ever seen a man move that fast.' By the time he was done, Brown added: 'I don't think Mick [Jagger] wanted to go on stage.'

Around the time that Brown found the tune, pianist Oscar Peterson also recorded it, for the 1962 album *Night Train*. Jimmy Forrest himself made a new arrangement with the Count Basie Orchestra, captured in 1979 in *Last of the Blue Devils*. Covers of 'Night Train' veered from ska, including Byron Lee's 1964 version, to the sedate country swing of Nashville pianist Floyd Cramer in 1967. But most ignored Brown's rhythmic daring. Indeed the song became a staple on the function band circuit, and was performed as such in the high school hop scene in the 1985 film *Back to the Future*.

Brown's serious intent, however, was never entirely cast aside. The glides, spins and splits of his stage routine inspired Michael Jackson's dance moves. Brown's version became a mod classic, propelling it on to the soundtrack of The Who's 1979 film *Quadrophenia.* The World Saxophone Quartet used Brown's rhythms as a platform for phonics and growls on their 1989 cover. Among those sampling and remixing Brown's 'Night Train', rap group Public Enemy's version on the album *Apocalypse 91* captures both venom and bite: the raw side of the song had won out.

Mike Hobart

18

BRIDGE OVER
TROUBLED WATER

In 2014, the British estate agent Savills advertised a property for sale, 'a picturesque thatched house' in the Devon village of Bickleigh. The listing stated: 'The pretty gardens extend along the river bank to Bickleigh Bridge, beside which the Simon and Garfunkel song "Bridge Over Troubled Water" is said to have been written.'

The Bickleigh Bridge story is an endearing and enduring tale – but it is entirely false. It's claimed that the song emerged from Paul Simon's stay at the nearby Fisherman's Cot inn when the river flooded in the 1960s. And it's true that Simon lived for a while in that part of Devon in the 1960s, and that he may even have stayed in Bickleigh. But in 2002, when Art Garfunkel was asked on BBC Radio Devon if the Bickleigh Bridge story was true, he replied, 'No, I'm sorry. "Bridge Over Troubled Water" is a gospel phrase which Paul took from a gospel group.'

The song was written by Simon in the rather less bucolic location of Los Angeles in 1969, partly inspired, as Garfunkel said, by the 1940s–50s gospel band The Swan Silvertones. During the recording sessions for what was to become Simon and Garfunkel's last album, tensions between the two men were running high, and Garfunkel was often away in Mexico filming *Catch-22* – absences that prompted Simon to write 'The Only Living Boy in New York'.

The sessions featured three musicians known as the 'Hollywood Golden Trio': bassist Joe Osborn, who gave the song its distinctive twin bass guitars; drummer Hal Blaine; and keyboardist Larry Knechtel. The song had been written on guitar in a different key and was arranged for piano by Jimmy Haskell.

To begin with, 'Bridge Over Troubled Water' was a modest affair with two verses, but Garfunkel thought that it had the potential to become something bigger; thus Simon came up with the third 'Sail on, silver girl' verse. The suggestion that this is a reference to drugs and needles is another myth: it was actually inspired by the premature grey hairs that had appeared on the head of Simon's then wife, Peggy Harper.

Placing the drums in an echo chamber and adding strings, producer Roy Halee transformed Simon's modest hymn into a grand, stirring Phil Spector-ish number. But who was to sing it? When it came to the vocals, which were recorded in New York, Simon thought it suited Garfunkel's voice; Garfunkel thought it was better suited to Simon's falsetto. Eventually Garfunkel relented and sang it. Simon has since said that he regretted 'giving the song away', not least because when they performed it live, Simon had to sit on the sidelines and watch Garfunkel lapping up the applause. It's ironic that a hymn to friendship and sacrifice turned out to be a source of resentment and jealousy between two old high-school friends.

'Bridge' became one of the biggest pop songs of 1970, charting at Number 1 on both sides of the Atlantic, while the album of the same title became a fixture at the top of the charts. Hundreds of versions followed (the Second Hand Songs website has counted more than 200). Elvis Presley included a grandiose, somewhat plodding live version on his 1970 album *Elvis: That's the Way It Is*. Jamaican singer Jimmy London reggaefied it. Willie Nelson countrified it with his customary elegance.

Both Simon and Garfunkel have continued to sing it; in 2015 Simon and Sting toured together, with Sting giving the song a powerful rendition. Not all versions were as respectful of the original: in 2008 Simon sued the Rhythm Watch Co of Japan for unlicensed use of the song on its 'Grand Nostalgia' musical clock, settling out of court for an undisclosed sum.

Perhaps the finest version was released in 1971 by Roberta Flack, whose arrangement took the song back to its roots with a gospelly, three-four swing. Over seven minutes, Flack inhabits the song (like many singers, she changes 'water' to 'waters') in a stunning vocal performance, with the Newark Boys Chorus adding an ethereal glow. It's music to ease a troubled mind.

David Cheal

19

YOU'RE SO VAIN

'I can't possibly tell who it's about because it wouldn't be fair,' Carly Simon told *Rolling Stone* magazine following the release of 1972's 'You're So Vain', adding, tantalizingly: 'I had about two or three people in mind.' And so began one of the great mysteries of modern pop.

Exquisitely acerbic and instantly catchy, 'You're So Vain' would turn out to be the biggest hit of Simon's career. It was a shoo-in for mainstream radio, though its lyrical bluntness about a man who 'had one eye in the mirror' was, at that time, unusual. This was a song written and performed by a woman, not only mocking an ex-lover for his colossal ego but candidly referencing sex ('You had me several years ago, when I was still quite naive').

Before her marriage to the singer James Taylor, Simon had had a number of affairs with well-known actors and musicians. Thus a handful of candidates were mooted as the song's protagonist, among them Cat Stevens, Kris Kristofferson, Warren Beatty and Mick Jagger. One Los Angeles disc jockey was so intrigued that he asked listeners to call in and vote on whom they thought it was about. Simon sagely kept schtum, though in 2003 she held a charity auction where she sold his identity to the highest bidder; the winner was Dick Ebersol, then chairman of NBC Sports, who paid $50,000 and was legally bound not to spill the beans.

It wasn't until 2015, when Simon published her memoir *Boys in the Trees*, that she confirmed what many had guessed: it was Warren Beatty who 'played second base in this particular infield, which he knows so well, but as for who manned first and third – ask the shortstop'. Earlier this year she unveiled a fourth verse to the song that never made the final cut, but which hinted that one of them was an adulterer. Truly, 'You're So Vain' is the gift that keeps on giving.

The track appears on the singer's third LP, *No Secrets*, which topped the US Billboard 200 and made her a global star. As a single, 'You're So Vain' (the original title was 'Ballad of a Vain Man') went to Number 1 and also earned her a Grammy nomination. Simon, who started out as a folk artist alongside her sister Lucy, wasn't happy with the raw, slightly rocky direction at first and clashed with producer Richard Perry over it. It was only when she heard it on the radio while sitting in a New York taxi that she conceded he was right.

While recording in London, Simon and Perry had earmarked Harry Nilsson for backing vocals. Nilsson duly arrived and began singing with Simon but, mid-session, Mick Jagger arrived and joined them in the vocal booth. Nilsson swiftly absented himself, saying: 'You two do not need me. You sound as though you're joined at the hip.' Jagger's vocals remained, though Simon insists rumours of their affair were unfounded.

'You're So Vain' has since proved inspirational for artists looking to rebuke ex-lovers: Janet Jackson's 2001 track 'Son of a Gun' borrowed a line from the chorus, while Taylor Swift, the reigning queen of the lyrical smackdown, sang it in Massachusetts during her 2013 *Red* tour, bringing Simon on to duet with her. Recorded covers have been plentiful but poor. In the mid-1990s The Mountain Goats reworked it as a pastoral, acoustic number,

stripping it of all passion in the process, and though Susanna Hoffs and Matthew Sweet did a better job for their 2009 *Under the Covers Vol. 2* LP, it still lacked the wounded ire of the original. Three years later, Marilyn Manson gave it the none-too-subtle industrial rock treatment, with Johnny Depp on guitar.

Ultimately, only Simon's version could rise to the challenge of accompanying a 2016 anti-Trump video from the political organization Patriotic Artists & Creatives, released on the eve of the second presidential debate, and on which she adjusted the line 'your scarf it was apricot' to 'your face it was apricot'. It's no small achievement that, 44 years on, Simon's most famous song continues to deliver well-aimed potshots at powerful, vainglorious men.

Fiona Sturges

20

MR TAMBOURINE MAN

It is one of the signature songs of the 1960s, the moment when the 'voice of a generation' (an epithet Bob Dylan always loathed) broke free of the strictures of folky protest to find himself in surrealistic poetry. Druggie anthem or search for the muse – it has been interpreted as both – the most important legacy of 'Mr Tambourine Man' is that it threw open the possibilities of what pop, and specifically pop lyrics, could be. That it was covered almost immediately by The Byrds – in a rockier version as influential as Dylan's acoustic original – only redoubles its impact.

Dylanologists date the initial writing to February 1964. The 22-year-old had been up all night at Mardi Gras in New Orleans. In that in-between time at the crack of dawn, he first caught those 'vague traces of skipping reels of rhyme' and, he later declared, 'the sound of what I wanted to say'. Too much can be read into his imagery yet it's a fair bet that Dylan's 'trip upon a magic swirling ship' is a reference to the French symbolist poet Rimbaud's 'Le Bateau Ivre' and the idea that inspiration can come via a 'systematic derangement of the senses'.

More prosaically, Mr Tambourine Man himself is probably just a bloke with a large percussion instrument. Dylan remembers Bruce Langhorne, whose electric guitar accompanies the singer on his definitive take, carrying a tambourine 'as big as a wagon wheel' around Greenwich Village. Thus he named the

Pied Piper-ish figure that the protagonist pursues in the 'jingle-jangle morning'.

The song was premiered at a Royal Festival Hall gig in London in May 1964. Dylan also played it at the Newport Folk Festival, and you can find a lovely film of that performance on YouTube. In June of 1964, he recorded the song with Ramblin' Jack Elliott. This version wasn't up to much but is now anthologized on the seventh of the *Bootleg Series*. Having therefore missed inclusion on 1964's *Another Side of . . .* album, 'Mr Tambourine Man' would eventually open the acoustic side of *Bringing It All Back Home*, the 1965 release that launched Dylan's 'electric' period and triggered an arms race of creativity with The Beatles and The Beach Boys.

The Byrds, meanwhile, also signed to Columbia, were encouraged to cover 'Mr Tambourine Man' as their debut single. The group, comprising Jim McGuinn, David Crosby, Gene Clark, Chris Hillman and Michael Clarke, were only convinced their version would fly when Dylan, hearing them play it live in the studio, exclaimed, 'Wow, man, you can dance to that!' Their rendition, however, nearly didn't get off the ground, as the producer, Doris Day's son Terry Melcher, wasn't happy with the twisted martial beat of their demo. Thinking the band's musical abilities weren't yet up to scratch, he brought in the peerless LA session musicians known later as the Wrecking Crew, and in particular Hal Blaine on drums. On 25 January 1965 (ten days after Dylan had cut his album version), McGuinn nailed his vocal and played the introduction on his 12-string Rickenbacker guitar. The heady sound kicked off the folk-rock boom. With abridged lyrics, and harmonies from McGuinn, Crosby and Gene Clark, these three minutes translated into a Number 1 on both sides of the pond.

As for his view of the song's meaning, McGuinn, who had changed his first name to Roger as a devotee of Subud, the Indonesian-derived spiritual sect, would describe it as 'a prayer of submission'. 'I was singing to God,' he professed, 'and I was saying to Him, "Hey, God, take me for a trip and I'll follow you anywhere".' If we can't vouch for any religious conversions, the flock of bands following his sonic lead include Big Star, The Smiths, REM, The Stone Roses and Teenage Fanclub.

Other performers have covered 'Mr Tambourine Man', notoriously William Shatner (aka *Star Trek*'s Captain Kirk) among them. To say their takes are inessential is an understatement. The most radical refashioning of Dylan's lyrics is by the classical composer John Corigliano, who set the words for soprano and orchestra in 2003 without having heard the original music.

Yet the most telling thing about the song's greatness is that Dylan maintains it's the only one of his songs he's tried to 'do another of' in the same vein. He failed, which shows how uniquely successful he was in the first place.

Richard Clayton

21

I AM THE WALRUS

It all started with a piece of fan mail. Well, fan mail and copious amounts of psychedelic drugs.

In 1967 John Lennon received a letter from a student at his old secondary school informing him that The Beatles' lyrics were being drily analysed in English class. Bemused, Lennon set about writing a song so chock full of arbitrarily chosen images and recherché references that it would be completely impervious to meaningful interpretation; 'Let the f***ers work that one out!' a bullish Lennon allegedly told a friend after penning a particularly convoluted verse.

Lennon already had the first two lines when he received the letter. The first, 'I am he as you are he as you are me and we are all together', a kind of Derridean chain of deferred meaning, came to the songwriter during an LSD trip. The second, 'See how they run like pigs from a gun', emerged during another narcotics-fuelled haze. The rest of the song was filled in later, and, some half a century on, this, one of the most enigmatic songs in The Beatles' canon ('Revolution 9' is unsurpassably strange), still perplexes.

The lyrics draw on the literary – Lennon was inspired by Lewis Carroll's nonsense poem 'The Walrus and the Carpenter' – the salacious – 'the eggman' referenced in the chorus alludes to an egg-based fetish indulged by The Animals' frontman, Eric Burdon – and everything in-between.

But an enduring fixation with the inscrutable lyrics means that the song's musical achievements are often overlooked. With 'I Am the Walrus', The Beatles, along with producer George Martin – who was apparently appalled by an early acoustic version of the track – came up with a dizzying, disorientating sonic experience not unlike the earlier 'Lucy in the Sky With Diamonds'. But where the latter had a dreamlike quality, here the effect verges on nightmarish.

The strings in the orchestral arrangement create an unbalanced tension as the notes rise and plummet. Lennon's vocals – sleazy, distorted and gravelly – help turn an absurdist exercise into a veritable rock anthem. An outlier among the more sing-songy, Paul McCartney-penned tracks on 1967's *Magical Mystery Tour*, it stands as a symbol of the ever-widening gulf in the songwriters' styles that would eventually tear the band apart three years later.

Many saw 1990s Britpop pioneers Oasis as the natural successors to The Beatles' legacy, and the Mancunian rockers adopted 'I Am the Walrus' as a staple of their live shows. Their version, featured on a deluxe edition of their *Definitely Maybe* album, is largely faithful, but the sprawling guitar solos detract from the original's punchiness. That said, Liam Gallagher, who modelled everything from his nasal voice to his look, on Lennon, performs the track with fitting impudence.

In 2007, U2's Bono recorded a version in-character for The Beatles musical film *Across the Universe*. The Irish frontman brings his best lung-busting arena-rock vocals to this cover, but his clean-cut voice and upstanding public image seem ill-fitting for a song that is absolutely dripping with manic seediness.

By sharp contrast, the song was also frequently covered by one of the biggest, zaniest personalities in rock, Frank Zappa, in his live concerts. In one especially surreal recording uploaded to YouTube, a visibly dazed Zappa takes an on-stage cigarette break and hands vocal duties over to a singer who holds a stuffed toy walrus aloft throughout the song.

In 2011 American indie rockers The Flaming Lips recorded a slightly sinister version, slower and even more distorted than the original. The video features lead man Wayne Coyne singing through a plastic plate and a backing musician (inexplicably wrapped in tinfoil) mimicking the complex orchestration with his voice.

Arguably the only version that can really sit alongside The Beatles' for the sheer entertainment and bewilderment it elicits is by Canadian comic actor Jim Carrey for George Martin's much-derided 1998 covers album *In My Life*. Carrey, an unexpectedly adept singer, really commits to the song, adding improvisational flourishes along the way to make the song his own – or, as he put it, 'defile a timeless piece of art'.

What all of these covers have in common is that they trade on the original track's inherent sense of playfulness. But the walrus would reappear in Lennon's work in a far more serious guise. In his 1970 polemical song, 'God', from his first solo album *John Lennon/Plastic Ono Band*, the singer declares: 'I was the walrus, but now I'm John.' It was an unexpectedly heart-rending way for him to renounce both The Beatles and his own anarchic spirit.

Dan Einav

22

WILD THING

In 1964, American songwriter Chip Taylor was in a New York recording studio with a new song gestating in his head. Taylor was ordinarily in the country and western business but he'd been asked to come up with a rock'n'roll song for a group called The Wild Ones. Time was tight; they only had about 15 minutes. 'I asked the engineer to turn the lights out so I could just lose myself in the song,' he told the BBC in 2013, 'and I just sang whatever came to mind and pictured myself with the person I was thinking about.'

The result was 'Wild Thing', a song that achieved distinction in an era of elemental riffs ('Louie Louie', 'I Can't Explain', 'You Really Got Me') and which journeyed effortlessly to and fro across the Atlantic. It also marked a turning point in the career of the greatest guitarist who ever lived: Jimi Hendrix.

To begin with, 'Wild Thing' struggled to be heard. The Wild Ones recorded it with a louche, garage-band swing and a harmonica solo, but it failed to chart. Then, in circumstances that are still disputed, the song found its way into the hands of The Troggs, the British band led by the implausibly-monikered Reg Presley (real name Reginald Ball). Bingo. Taylor's primal riff was a perfect match for a band whose name was an abbreviation of 'troglodyte'.

In 1966 'Wild Thing' reached the top of the US charts and

Number 2 in the UK, and Presley was able to give up his day job as a bricklayer. The song's prehistoric atmosphere was accentuated by its use of an ocarina solo. Taylor's original demo had featured a sound engineer whistling through his hands, but The Troggs chose to use this ancient wind instrument, a kind of shepherd's flute, whose limited range adds to the song's potency. This was the sound of the stone age, filtered through the raw sexuality of the 1960s.

In the intervening years, according to National Public Radio, more than 7,500 licences have been issued for recordings by the song's publisher. But none has been more momentous than Jimi Hendrix's version. In the mid-1960s Hendrix had been incubated in London by his manager Chas Chandler, in a musical culture that seemed more receptive to the idea of a black rock guitarist. But in June 1967 Chandler decided that the US was ready for Hendrix and booked him a slot at the Monterey Pop Festival.

At Chandler's suggestion, Hendrix had already set fire to his guitar at the Astoria Theatre in London (later the Rainbow) while performing his song 'Fire', sustaining burns that had to be treated in hospital. But when he did it on stage at Monterey during 'Wild Thing', it made national headlines (and Hendrix this time avoided injury). In these days of stadium pyrotechnics and megawatt light shows, a man kneeling on stage squirting lighter fuel over his burning Fender Stratocaster might seem quaint. But Hendrix's climactic antics, playing his guitar behind his back, riffing and soloing with insouciant genius, laying his guitar out like a sacrificial victim, gesturing with his hands like a shaman as the flames consume his instrument and weird sounds crackle from its frazzled pick-ups, and finally smashing it to pieces while Noel Redding and Mitch Mitchell whump and clatter on bass and drums: the whole thing is electrifying. It's not hyperbolic to say that 'Wild Thing' made Hendrix in the US.

Meanwhile, a very different version of 'Wild Thing' was circulating in the US. In an early example of media-aware satire, in 1967 comedian Bill Minkin imitated Bobby Kennedy, playing the part of the senator during a recording session as he essays a comically stilted spoken version of 'Wild Thing' while a producer and an adviser urge him to relax into the song ('That's it, senator, groove with it'). It sold hundreds of thousands.

But perhaps the most striking of those 7,500-odd licensed recordings is a 1981 version by The Creatures (Budgie and Siouxsie Sioux from Siouxsie and the Banshees), on which Siouxsie's chilly multitracked vocals (at one point she chants 'Wild thing, I think I hate you') are accompanied only by Budgie's tribal-sounding drums. It's a version that taps into the earthy, elemental spirit of the song, channelling those few minutes back in 1964 when Chip Taylor lost himself in the darkness of a New York studio.

David Cheal

23

TIME AFTER TIME

Cyndi Lauper didn't plan to write 'Time after Time' at all. The New York-raised singer had already left the recording studio after – she thought – completing her first solo album, *She's So Unusual*. Released in 1983, it went on to produce four Top 5 singles, and a Grammy in 1984 for best new artist. But before any of that, Lauper's producer reckoned the album was coming in one number short, and could she please turn in another track?

She and her co-writer, keyboardist Rob Hyman, returned to the studio. Lauper flicked through a TV guide hoping that some title or other might jump out and kickstart a new song. One of them did: a listing for *Time after Time*, a 1979 film starring Malcolm McDowell as H.G. Wells in pursuit of Jack the Ripper, who has hijacked his time machine.

Lauper and Hyman dispensed with the film's plot, coming up instead with a 1980s-defining romantic ballad that distilled the contradictory emotions of an unwinding relationship into four minutes of brilliantly conceived narrative pop. Here, a young woman moves on – not dumped – from a relationship that she still treasures: 'If you're lost you can look – and you will find me / time after time / if you fall I will catch you, I'll be waiting, time after time.'

Her record label wanted 'Time After Time' as the album's lead single, but Lauper feared being typecast as a balladeer. The proto-girl power anthem 'Girls Just Want to Have Fun' was released instead, catapulting Lauper into the charts and all over MTV. 'Time After Time' and its semi-autobiographical video followed.

Lauper was perfect for the early years of MTV, or perhaps MTV was perfect for her. She wore her hair wild and crimson, or pink, or purple; her clothes were a mad era-hopping thrift-store explosion of colour and defiant mismatch that didn't need a fat wallet and a thin body. In 1984 she told *Rolling Stone* magazine: 'People used throw rocks at me for my clothes. Now they wanna know where I buy them.'

Confident and iconoclastic, Lauper influenced a line of female singers, from Madonna to Alanis Morissette and Britney Spears. But it was about more than her look. She was a genuine musi-cian, with a four-octave range that she sometimes deployed in seemingly casual near-cartoonish ways. The lyrics to 'Time After Time' border on the poetic, and Lauper's rhythmically delivered post-punk vocals, fitting with sparse drums, swirly keyboards and a light, slow-reggae beat, combine into a powerfully affecting force.

Artists queued up to perform the song, its dozens of covers ranging from Paul Anka's brassy swing band account to versions by Pink, Leona Lewis, and the London Symphony Orchestra. But the one that Lauper said made her happiest came from jazz trumpeter Miles Davis, whose then-wife, the actress Cicely Tyson, suggested the song to him.

Davis had lit on the idea of an album of covers of contem-porary pop ballads, with arrangements by long-time associate Gil Evans. Davis recorded demos of 40 ballad covers, including 'Time After Time'. But the project collapsed when he broke his hip and then succumbed to pneumonia.

By the time Davis returned to the recording studio his focus had radically shifted – 1985's album *You're Under Arrest* was an eclectic mix of pop, politics, heavy funk and reggae. But 'Time After Time' was retained, becoming one of the first successful jazz covers of a new-wave pop song, foreshadowing a practice that took 20 years to become commonplace.

Davis's wistful instrumental interpretation captured the bittersweet mood of Lauper's lyrics. It became a repertory highlight through to his final public performance, at the Hollywood Bowl in August 1991. *The Complete Miles Davis at Montreux 1973–1991* CD set, showcasing his appearances at the Swiss festival, contains no fewer than nine versions of 'Time after Time', none of them under eight minutes long.

Lauper's hit now stands as a kind of aural shorthand for the 1980s. The Netflix series *Stranger Things* concluded its second season with a school dance: it's 1984 and – of course – 'Time after Time' is the smoochy number.

But *Stranger Things* is not the only weird-goings-on outing for the Lauper classic. The original Malcolm McDowell film was remade as a television series and shown in the US in 2017, until ABC axed it mid-run. A plaintive Change.Org online petition put out a plea for Netflix to pick the season up and revive it – perhaps with a view to making it through to the end of the song, for the series uses lines from the titular single as episode titles. It was dumped at episode five: 'Picture fades'.

Mike Hobart

SHE'S LOST CONTROL

In 1978, for those who cared to listen, a chilly, stripped-down sound could be heard in the north of England, signalling a new direction. Manchester's Joy Division performed 'She's Lost Control' for the first time in June that year, playing to audiences of a few hundred people. The song appeared on their 1979 debut album, *Unknown Pleasures*, and was re-recorded for the B-side of their 1980 single 'Atmosphere'.

This strange, dark song has intrigued artists and producers worldwide. It provided the title for Anton Corbijn's 2007 Joy Division biopic *Control*. Many have covered it and repurposed its lyrics. Vocalist Ian Curtis sounded like the oldest soul. That such cold, forbidding vocals could come from a young man with lowered eyes, plain clothes and an odd, angular dance made them even eerier. According to Peter Hook, the band's bassist, Joy Division's aim was to emulate the Sex Pistols, but they ended up sounding like nothing else; Hook credits producer Martin Hannett with conjuring their arid, industrial sonics.

The lyrics, with their unsettling narrative about a woman's physical – or mental – collapse, were written by Curtis. They would prove horribly portentous. Curtis held down a day job in a Manchester employment exchange, where he found work for people with disabilities. One young woman was desperate to work, but suffered from epileptic seizures: every time she visited the exchange she would suffer a fit, which disturbed Curtis greatly. He wrote the song in response to her sudden death. Soon afterwards, the 21-year-old Curtis was diagnosed with epilepsy. Hook conjectures that Curtis suspected his condition when he wrote the lyrics, which may explain his empathy for the girl – though he kept it hidden from his bandmates. Curtis killed himself in 1980, an event that Hook blames in part on the stress of living with seizures.

Weeks later 'Love Will Tear Us Apart' was a posthumous breakthrough hit. Joy Division were broke. The band could only afford to practise for a few hours a week, and songs, including 'She's Lost Control', were necessarily written in haste and existed only when all four members came together. Even a tape recorder was beyond their means.

When Grace Jones covered the song in 1980, the bewildered band received £5,000, which seemed to them a fortune. Jones's version, with lyrics adjusted to a female perspective, was released in 1980 as a B-side to another cover, the Pretenders' 'Private Life'. She recorded her version in the Bahamas at Compass Point Studios, backed by the house band, which included production duo Sly Dunbar and Robbie Shakespeare. Hook's desolate bassline remains, but is repurposed into a squelchy reggae riff. Jones remembers in her autobiography that the song was among several chosen by Chris Blackwell, owner of Island records, and his team; the covers were designed to redirect her career from New York disco to an international audience.

Jones recalls that she interpreted the song literally. 'I lost control to such an extent that I scared myself . . . As far as I was concerned it was a self-portrait.' In contrast to Curtis's third-person narrative, Jones's version is about herself. While

his performance is restrained, her vocals are deranged. The song was an ingenious choice for an artist whose persona is defined by control.

Since then there have been some less celebrated covers, including Greek new wave band Alive She Died, whose mid-1980s recording was used by Gucci in a recent advertising campaign, and by the group Shakespears Sister in 2004.

Perhaps the most innovative interpretation came from Soweto in 2010. Spoek Mathambo, a South African artist and producer, is a Joy Division fan drawn to the 'dark and uplifting' quality of UK late-1970s punk and new wave. He draws parallels with South African electronic music – both, he says, express a dark time while offering transcendent relief. He wrote a half-cover and renamed it 'Control': the lyrics hint at the original but, he says, were intended to convey the collapse of a relationship.

Hook now performs 'She's Lost Control' with his band, Peter Hook & the Light. In 2016, he played the song in Buenos Aires: 'Watching thousands singing along is so strange . . . it's dark, people adore that.'

Helen Barrett

JE T'AIME . . . MOI NON PLUS

By the time Brigitte Bardot began dating Serge Gainsbourg, the 34-year-old film siren had grown cynical of conventional romance. Her third husband, millionaire playboy Gunter Sachs, had showered her home with hundreds of roses from his helicopter before they married in 1966. But by 1967 he was cheating. Gainsbourg, the 39-year-old composer who joked he had a 'head like a cabbage', developed an obsession with 'BB'. He signed her to the record label on which he pumped out perky pop hits and took her out after the pair had appeared on a TV show together.

Alas a combination of awe and booze caused Gainsbourg's celebrated wit and charm to desert him and he staggered home believing he'd blown it. But the next day Bardot called offering him a second chance, on condition that he write her 'the most beautiful love song he could imagine'. Ever excessive, he wrote two: 'Bonnie and Clyde' and 'Je t'aime . . . moi non plus'.

Although the sweet, swirling organ melody of 'Je t'aime' (which echoed that summer's big hit, Procol Harum's 'A Whiter Shade of Pale': see Chapter 45) met Bardot's demand for beauty, the lyrics must have given her pause. The drunken provocateur who had just fluffed their date was asking her to sigh that she loved him while he would reply, deadpan: 'Me neither'. Gainsbourg's love of rhyme also led him to locate the act of love 'between your kidneys': 'Je vais et je viens / Entre tes reins.'

But Gainsbourg's musings on the hopelessness of love struck a chord with the restless and troubled Bardot. They became lovers and met in Paris that winter to squeeze into an increasingly steamy booth and record 'Je t'aime'. The French press got wind of the recording and whipped up a scandal, suggesting the couple had had sex while making it. Bardot fretted that the bad publicity would damage her career and persuaded Gainsbourg to shelve the recording. He was frustrated. 'The music is very pure,' he said. 'For the first time in my life I write a love song, and what happens? They take it the wrong way.'

He approached other women, including Marianne Faithfull, to take Bardot's part but in 1968 convinced his new girlfriend, English actress Jane Birkin, to do the heavy breathing. Gainsbourg laughed off further rumours of audio vérité: 'Thank goodness it wasn't, otherwise I hope it would have been a long-playing record.' Despite being banned by the BBC and condemned by the Vatican, the song shifted millions around the world and shot to Number 1 in the UK where its lyrical subtleties were lost in translation; it became a straightforward disco snogging song.

That Christmas, Birkin played the rest of the couple's debut album to her family, but decided to spare them her orgasmic groans. Meanwhile Birkin's brother, Andrew, later said that the former Nazi armaments minister Albert Speer had asked him for a signed copy of the record, an irony which delighted the Jewish Gainsbourg.

A slew of suggestive spoofs followed from comics including Frankie Howerd, June Whitfield and a version packed with 'Gud moaning' from the cast of the British sitcom 'Allo 'Allo, set in Nazi-occupied Paris. The song's breathy sensuality helped inspire Donna Summer and Giorgio Moroder's pulsating disco sound and they covered it together, with added sax appeal, in 1978. Artist Sam Taylor-Wood swapped the word 'kidneys' for 'thighs' in an English-language version with the Pet Shop Boys (1998) that cleverly evoked the digital despair of internet porn. Cat Power and Karen Elson swung it smartly Sapphic in 2008 while Madonna gave it a melodramatic S&M twist on her 2012 *MDMA* tour. Birkin references it on *Birkin/Gainsbourg: le Symphonique*, a Serge Gainsbourg covers album, which she released in 2017.

Bardot finally released the original in 1986 to raise funds for her animal charities. 'I gave my beauty and youth to men,' she said. 'Now I am giving my wisdom and experience – the best of me – to animals.' At the end of her affair with Gainsbourg, while he filled her suitcase with love letters, Bardot pierced the skin of her right index finger and wrote 'I love you' in blood. He did the same and wrote 'Me neither'.

Helen Brown

MACK THE KNIFE

At the heart of the story of 'Mack the Knife' is a great irony: a song about a cold-blooded serial murderer written by a Marxist playwright and a leftwing composer for a musical that aimed to lay bare the hypocrisies of bourgeois morality went on to become a huge commercial success globally, especially in the US. It was even used in a 1980s advertising campaign for McDonald's hamburgers ('Mac tonight').

Bertolt Brecht and Kurt Weill's *The Threepenny Opera*, which was based on John Gay's *The Beggar's Opera* of 1728, opened in Berlin in 1928. Brecht and Weill's work sets the action in Victorian London where the villain, Macheath, goes about his dastardly business. With only a few days to go before the show opened at the Theater am Schiffbauerdamm (featuring Weill's wife Lotte Lenya as Jenny Diver), the production's egotistical star Harold Paulsen, playing Mackie, insisted that he be given a grand introduction. So Brecht and Weill quickly wrote a scene-setting *Moritat* (murder ballad), with barrel-organ accompaniment, bigging up the dreadful deeds of Mackie Messer ('Mack the Knife').

Audiences were slow to respond to a show that was neither musical nor opera but a new, jazz-influenced amalgam. However, *The Threepenny Opera* eventually caught on and was performed more than 400 times in the next two years. The rise of Hitler forced Brecht and Weill into exile; in 1938 Weill was labelled a composer of 'degenerate music' in the Düsseldorf exhibition that followed the previous year's show of 'degenerate art'.

After the Second World War *The Threepenny Opera* crossed the Atlantic, running in 1952 at Brandeis University, Massachusetts, conducted by Leonard Bernstein (with lyrics translated into English by Marc Blitzstein), before opening off-Broadway in 1954 (again featuring Lenya). In its passage to the US, something happened to 'Mack the Knife': where the German-language original has a dirge-like quality, in the US it became the jaunty tale of a roguish gangster.

It was Louis Armstrong who pushed 'Mack the Knife' into the jazz repertoire in 1955, having been encouraged by a Columbia Records executive to cover it, and he established the template for versions that followed. Some of Mackie's deeds were omitted – the original tells of a woman being raped by Mackie in her sleep. Nevertheless, Blitzstein's translated lyric is brilliantly vivid: 'Scarlet billows start to spread.' The word 'dear' (and, later, 'babe') was added to help the lyrics to scan. Armstrong also ad-libbed a mention of Lotte Lenya to the song's roll-call of victims, and her name has stuck ever since.

In 1959 Bobby Darin took the song by the scruff of the neck and turned it into the swing classic widely known today. Unlike the Brecht–Weill original, which remains in the same key throughout, Darin's version changes key, chromatically, no fewer than five times, ratcheting up the tension.

By now the song had become a standard, open to all-comers including Frank Sinatra and Peggy Lee. Ella Fitzgerald and Duke Ellington recorded a blistering version at the Jazz à Juan Festival in 1966; as well as scatting sensationally, Fitzgerald trumps Darin with 11 key changes. Notable German-language versions,

meanwhile, were performed by Lotte Lenya herself back in the 1930s, and more recently by Ute Lemper, whose sinister reading features a cascade of rolled Germanic 'r's. Nick Cave recorded a memorably chilling version; he sings in English but references the song's German roots with his oompah arrangement.

But a real flavour of the song's origins can be found in GW Pabst's 1931 film of *The Threepenny Opera*. As Mackie skulks among the crowds, our singer–narrator – using a kind of flip-chart of Mackie's crimes – intones the song with deadpan dread, to the mournful, scraping accompaniment of the barrel-organ. Here, Mackie is no caricature gangster but a nasty piece of work.

David Cheal

WILL YOU LOVE ME TOMORROW

It was released in the same year as the first oral contraceptive pill, and few songs have captured the bitter-sweetness of a cultural revolution more perfectly than 'Will You Love Me Tomorrow', which Carole King and Gerry Goffin wrote for The Shirelles in 1960.

King and Goffin had married hastily in 1958 after King became pregnant aged 17, and Goffin was still working at a chemical company when the Brill Building's 'Man with the Golden Ear', Don Kirshner, commissioned the ambitious duo to write something for the up-and-coming New Jersey doo-woppers. One of the few girl groups to compose their own material, The Shirelles needed a follow-up to their minor 1960 hit 'Tonight's the Night', which saw lead vocalist Shirley Owens torn over a lover's offer to 'turn the lights down low' and make her 'feel all aglow / Well I don't know . . . You might break my heart.'

Goffin and King were so excited they simply continued the narrative. King bashed out the melody in an afternoon (with their infant daughter in a playpen beside the piano), then dashed out to play mah-jong with a friend, leaving a note for her husband near the tape recorder reading: 'Please write'.

'I listened to it a few times,' Goffin told King's biographer, Sheila Weller, 'then I put myself in the place of a woman – yes, it was sort of autobiographical. I thought: what would a girl sing to a guy if they made love that night?'

In just a few simple lines, Goffin nailed the insecurities of a new generation of sexually liberated women. He wrote for a voice that was confident and vulnerable in equal measure: 'So tell me now and I won't ask again / Will you still love me tomorrow?'

The Shirelles originally thought the song sounded 'too country' for their urban, R&B style, but were won over by the addition of a dramatic string section. Owens's voice struck out deep and direct across the peppy beat of ambidextrous session drummer Gary Chester and the brisk sha-la-las of her former classmates. The single became the first US Number 1 for a black female group.

Although it was covered by The Four Seasons, Linda Ronstadt and Roberta Flack over the next decade, it was King's own 1971 recording that really moved the song on. One of only two old Goffin/King numbers to appear on her best-selling *Tapestry* album (which King performed live, in its entirety, for the first time in Hyde Park in July 2016), it was stripped of its youthful uncertainty and delivered from the wearier, wiser lips of a woman who had been burnt before. The studio lights were turned down low as fellow singer–songwriters Joni Mitchell and James Taylor sang backing vocals.

The song is now a classic of the female singer–songwriter canon: you can throw a heartbroken howl at it like Amy Winehouse (whose 2004 recording for the soundtrack of *Bridget Jones: The Edge of Reason* was vandalized by cheesy production including beach-bar bongos, and mercifully re-produced by Mark Ronson in 2011), whisper it like Norah Jones in 2009 or sob it (with menace) into your piano as Swedish indie-pop star

Lykke Li did for the soundtrack of Kimberly Peirce's 2013 *Carrie* remake.

Although it had been covered by men before, Bryan Ferry gave the song its most searching gender flip in 1993, his melancholy sighs floating over lonesome splashes of synth, an echoing guitar and ghostly atmospherics. Then in 2010, as scientists at Israel's Bar-Ilan University claimed to have developed the first male contraceptive pill, Kanye West lamented a world in which women could now use men as they had once been used. 'How she gon' wake up and not love me no more? / I thought I was the asshole, I guess it's rubbing off,' rapped Kanye on 'Devil in a New Dress' against a slickly seductive Smokey Robinson sample from 1973. What was Smokey singing? 'Will You Love Me Tomorrow'.

Helen Brown

(I CAN'T GET NO) SATISFACTION

In the mid-1960s there must have been something in the pillows. Famously, the melody of 'Yesterday' came to Paul McCartney in a dream. Early in 1965, in a Florida hotel, inspiration similarly struck a slumbering Keith Richards in the form of a five-note guitar riff. Waking, he hastily recorded it on reel-to-reel tape; then he went back to sleep.

Richards took the tape (two minutes of playing, he would say later, 'then me snoring for 40 minutes') to his bandmates and asked them the same question McCartney posed to his: was this an original fragment or simply cryptomnesia, a non-attributed memory? Slight chimes with Martha and the Vandellas' 'Nowhere to Run' aside, the riff was original enough and powerful enough to make a song.

Richards laid down fuzzed guitar as a marker for where he thought a Motown-style horn part should run. Rare stereo versions separate out the guitar lines so that you can hear the distorted line and an acoustic one run in tandem (and reveal Jack Nitzsche's piano); in the mono brutality of the released version the two become one. The guitar line comes and goes – at times it drops out so that the beat is kept solely by handclaps and drums hard on the beat, and then the riff nags back in.

The lyrics are often read as referring specifically to sexual frustration, Jagger rhyming 'satisfaction' with 'girl reaction' (it sounds as if he is singing about 'girly action', which is even worse), but the subject matter is wider than that. Most of the song is a rejection of the white heat of consumerism – an advertiser tells the narrator how white his shirts could be, and which brand of cigarette he should smoke. Jagger's verses are, literally, one note, a sort of drawled proto-rap, which makes the diminished arpeggio of the chorus all the more striking: a form of release that simultaneously bemoans its own lack of release. The sexual references in the third verse guaranteed the kind of controversy on which the band thrived, setting them up for censorship on television and radio and sending fans to the shops for a potent hit of danger.

'Satisfaction' was The Rolling Stones' first Number 1 in the US. It marked the point at which they moved away from being R&B copyists to the creators of bona fide classics. For many, it encapsulates not only the band but also the whole decade. When the BBC adapted Malcolm Bradbury's novel *The History Man* and wished to show the anti-hero, Howard Kirk, as a swaggering sexist out of his time, this was the song they put on his record player. It also marked the point at which Brian Jones, the band's founder, became peripheral to the Stones' future – even though it was he who insisted it should be a single. Half a century later, the song is still central to the Stones' sets: generally, it marks the point at which their concerts come to life. Satisfyingly enough, in 2016 Jagger became a father for the eighth time at the age of 73.

Cover versions of 'Satisfaction' abound: Britney Spears, Samantha Fox and Vanilla Ice have all weighed in. For such a celebrated song, though, surprisingly few covers come from actual heavyweights. Otis Redding's is at best an approximation of the lyrics, but he does have the bright, punchy horns of which Richards had dreamt. Devo, the Akron-based surrealist provocateurs, recorded a spiky, angular stab. Aretha Franklin, uncharacteristically, missed the point by sounding all-too satisfied. More recently, at the Brit Awards in 1994, PJ Harvey and Björk performed the song as a duet for ego and id. Björk was at her most gamine, Harvey at her most androgynous. Taking the lead vocal, Harvey flattened out the melody even more resolutely than Jagger, and slowed the guitar line down to a brutally clipped dry strum. Björk's backing vocals grew from growl to shriek, sounding increasingly unhinged. Once again, so many years on, the song sounded positively dangerous.

David Honigmann

29

TAINTED LOVE

The opening two notes of the song that helped define the 1980s synth-pop era are still one of the most instantly recognizable intros to any pop tune.

Yet Soft Cell's enduring 1981 multimillion-seller 'Tainted Love', which marked a guitar-ousting genre that dominated much of the decade, came from a cover version of a 1960s B-side by an American soul singer.

Gloria Jones, a one-time member of the Motown songwriting operation, recorded 'Tainted Love' in 1965 for LA writer and producer Ed Cobb. Jones's version is a terrific, stompingly break-neck burst of female had-it-up-to-here defiance. But it slipped past unnoticed until the early 1970s, when the mainly working-class British northern soul scene, devotees of obscure or rare black American soul music, fell in love with it. Northern soul clubs such as the Wigan Casino and Manchester's Twisted Wheel turned it into one of the most enduring, and most bootlegged, anthems of this passionately partisan scene.

But Jones, a preacher's daughter, said that she 'never really liked "Tainted Love".' Talking to *This Day in Music Radio*, the former church singer recalled: 'It didn't feel like something [that] could really present my style: I was more of a torch singer. And I didn't like the word "tainted". I felt it was vulgar and just wasn't proper.'

Jones also felt she should have shared writing credits, arguing that when Cobb brought the song to her she changed the melody. 'He never said, OK Gloria that will be 50 per cent, he was like, oh, thank you very much.'

Jones, who later joined the cast of the musical *Hair*, knew nothing of the song's underground success until, working as a backing singer for the UK glam-rock band T Rex, Marc Bolan asked her if she was 'the' Gloria Jones. The pair went on to live together until Bolan died in 1977, when the car Jones was driving crashed. The year before, Jones had re-recorded 'Tainted Love', though to negligible interest. Bolan himself produced a version of the song for Jones's 1976 album *Vixen*.

But it was the northern soul connection that in 1981 was to catapult 'Tainted Love' into a near-year-long chart residency. Soft Cell were then a little-known post-punk band, although they did have a recording deal. At the time vocalist Marc Almond was working in the cloakroom of Leeds club The Warehouse.

Warehouse DJ Ian Dewhirst had been a legendary rare vinyl hunter on the northern soul circuit, and put the Jones single on the turntable. Dewhirst later told writer Bill Brewster that 'this guy who I'd conspicuously avoided for nine months (he was always getting into fights with women or something) came rushing up . . . "What's this record? I've got to know what this record is!"'

The result of that chance hearing was Soft Cell's third single, its success fast and total. The metallic sound and the brassy electronic signature stabs that punctuate the number came from the duo's electronica and keyboard player David Ball, the big silent guy at the back (or 'the brickie', as pop mag *Smash Hits* called him), who was a perfect visual foil to the flamboyant Almond. The first run-through of Almond's deliberately

mannered, thrillingly sinister lead vocal, aimed at merely checking the sound, was the one that was used on the final cut.

American goth-rock singer Marilyn Manson picked up the song for a version in 2001 that was bombastic, trashy and just as absurd as a number on the soundtrack of a parodic film called *Not Another Teen Movie* should be. Rihanna sampled the opening notes of the Soft Cell version throughout her 2006 hit 'SOS'.

But surely the most inspired repurposing of those two notes belongs to Hollywood's Spike Jonze, director of *Being John Malkovich*. For a 1996 ad for Levi's jeans, Jonze set the action in a hospital emergency room, hooking the notes into the 'beep beep' of the monitors and setting medics and gas-and-air-addled patient into a delirious song-and-dance version – until the patient crashes. But – hurrah – he survives! Beep beep!

Sue Norris

30

WHEN THE LEVEE BREAKS

In December 1970 Led Zeppelin's drummer John Bonham had just taken delivery of a brand new Ludwig drum kit. It was about to get a hell of a hammering. He and the band were recording their fourth album at Headley Grange, a former poorhouse in Hampshire, and they were seeking a special kind of drum sound for a song called 'When the Levee Breaks': something big, something epic.

There's a long tradition of British recording artists employing a domestic approach to the creation of distinctive sonic effects: 1960s producer and songwriter Joe Meek (of 'Telstar' fame) used the bathroom of his rented flat on London's Holloway Road to record vocals; Ringo Starr stretched tea towels over his drums to achieve a muffled effect. Zeppelin's solution was to place the drum kit at the foot of Headley Grange's three-storey stairwell and hang microphones from the top, thus exploiting the structure's natural reverberative qualities.

The result is one of the heaviest – and most heavily sampled – drum tracks ever recorded: Bonham locks down a groove that is truly massive, his limbs pumping like steam-driven pistons as bass drum and snare whump and rattle, with the occasional splash of cymbal shimmering. And the track itself is one of Zeppelin's finest moments, a draggy, druggy haze of drums, guitar, vocals and backwards-recorded harmonica; a swirling, hypnotic vortex of heavily treated sound – no wonder they almost never played it live.

The song's origins, though, are more modest. Guitarist Jimmy Page had emerged from the British blues boom of the 1960s with The Yardbirds before forming Led Zeppelin in 1968, and 'When the Levee Breaks' – like a fair amount of Zeppelin's material – had its origins in the American blues: in this case, an old tune of the same title by Kansas Joe McCoy and Memphis Minnie; released in 1929, the duo's song recalls the devastating Mississippi floods of 1927. With its briskly strummed guitars, McCoy and Minnie's song has an almost jaunty quality that is at odds with its subject matter ('Mean ol' levee, cause me to weep and moan,' sings McCoy).

Zeppelin had got themselves into trouble on an earlier album by failing to properly credit Howlin' Wolf's 'Killing Floor' as a key component in 'The Lemon Song' (Wolf's music publisher sued; the parties settled out of court), and the band were dogged by accusations that they ripped off blues acts. In the case of 'When the Levee Breaks', though, the credits were given as Page/Plant/Jones/Bonham/Memphis Minnie.

The label for the 1929 Columbia disc of the song has a couple of bits of printed description: 'Guitar accomp.' and 'Electrical process'. But the real 'electrical process' came in the 1960s and early 1970s when bands such as Cream, John Mayall's Bluesbreakers, Fleetwood Mac and Zeppelin plugged the blues into the mains and broadcast it to a new audience of white kids. Essentially, what Zeppelin and the other British blues-based bands were doing was a kind of sampling: taking a song, or an element of a song, and working it into something radically new.

So there is a satisfying karmic circularity to the fact that

Bonham's drum track was subsequently picked up and sampled by dozens of US hip-hop acts, who clearly relished its pulverizing groove: The Beastie Boys on 'Rhymin' & Stealin' ' (1986); MC Lyte's 'Survival of the Fittest' (1989); Dr Dre on 'Lyrical Gangbang' from his 1992 album *The Chronic*; Eminem on 'Kim' (2000). (Bristol trip-hoppers Massive Attack also used it on 1998's 'Man Next Door'.) And all because, at Headley Grange in 1970, John Bonham had been stationed in a stairwell to musical heaven.

David Cheal

31

TUTTI FRUTTI

Richard Penniman was partway through another desultory recording session on 14 September 1955 when his producer, Robert 'Bumps' Blackwell, took the musicians to lunch at the Dew Drop Inn in New Orleans. Penniman, who recorded under the name Little Richard, took to the restaurant's piano and started hollering along with his own playing. His opening words, Blackwell later recalled, were 'A-wop-bop-a-loo-bop-a-good-God-damn!' and, the producer said, they were the only clean words in the song Richard bashed out.

Richard had been trying and failing to have hits for four years at this point, no studio or producer being able to capture his elemental, pansexual wildness. Everyone wanted to fit him to a template, but Richard fitted no templates. He was himself, or he was nothing. On hearing the nascent 'Tutti Frutti', Blackwell realized the errors that had been made before. Rather than trying to force Richard towards some different song entirely, he decided to focus and sharpen the Richard who had thought it appropriate to sing a song about anal sex ('If it don't fit, don't force it / You can grease it, make it easy' ran the original lyric) to a restaurant crowd.

He cajoled a writer called Dorothy LaBostrie into tidying up the lyric. She did so with 15 minutes to go in the afternoon session. In that quarter hour, Blackwell cut three takes of 'Tutti

Frutti', now about a girl who 'rocks to the east, she rocks to the west / She's the girl that I love best' and gave the world the ten much disputed syllables that are item one on the syllabus of rock'n'roll: 'Awopbopaloomopalopbombom!'

Even now, more than 60 years on, that Specialty Records recording of 'Tutti Frutti' still sounds wild to the point of being unhinged. Richard's voice is clearly hitting the red, clipping and distorting; the band sound like they're desperately trying to keep up; his piano sounds like it's playing itself; and punctuating it all are Richard's high whoops, copied incessantly by The Beatles on their early recordings.

It's a record so exciting, so primal, that it is both irresistible and insurrectionary. It is the sound of an incomprehensible force. Small wonder then, that despite it being a hit (Number 17 in the US), Pat Boone was corralled into recording a version in which any hint of sex was expunged from the performance, which reached Number 12 in early 1956. Quite how unsuitable Boone was to record 'Tutti Frutti' was shown in 1958, when he published *Twixt Twelve and Twenty*, his book of advice for young people. 'Kissing for fun is like playing with a beautiful candle in a room full of dynamite!' he suggested, words Richard would never have uttered, unless he were also demanding an explosion.

'Tutti Frutti' became the Ur-text of rock'n'roll. Although the rise of Chuck Berry and Buddy Holly saw the guitar replace the piano as the driving instrument of rock music, 'Tutti Frutti' was the song every aspirant swivel-hipped hero had to try. It was covered by the German Elvis, Peter Kraus; by the Italian Elvis, Adriano Celentano; by the French Elvis, Johnny Hallyday; and by the actual Elvis, on his 1956 debut album. Of those versions, the unfairly maligned Hallyday offers the best, tightening it into coiled R&B.

Even after The Beatles began the process of rendering the first wave of rock'n'roll obsolescent, 'Tutti Frutti' lived on. When a band wanted to prove their connection to the founding fathers of rock, 'Tutti Frutti' was the song they would turn to. The MC5 played it fast and tinny. Fleetwood Mac played it live, with a pointless dirge of a breakdown. Queen played it at every show of their *Magic* tour in 1986.

But no one else ever captured the lightning of the song the way Little Richard and Bumps Blackwell did in September 1955. 'Tutti Frutti' is more than a song; it's the thing that rock'n'roll is built on – a record. A record of a moment that could never be recaptured.

Michael Hann

32

IT'S A LONG WAY TO TIPPERARY

'You've come a long way,' reads the sign on Ireland's N24 as you enter Tipperary – a nod to the song that made the town famous during the First World War.

The myth is that 'It's a Long Way to Tipperary' was written solely by music hall entertainer Jack Judge in January 1912. Judge, a former fishmonger, liked to boast of how a fellow entertainer bet five shillings that he couldn't compose and sing a new song in 24 hours. By the following night, Judge claimed to have knocked out the new song and incorporated it into his act.

But it now seems more likely that the Worcestershire-born Judge had simply tinkered with an older number (about a home-sick Irish lad writing home to his sweetheart from London) called 'It's a Long Way to Connemara' that he had co-written in 1909 with Harry Williams, whose family ran a pub in Warwickshire.

Described by his great niece, Meg Pybus, as 'a sensitive and sickly man', Williams was a poet and multi-instrumentalist, confined to a wheelchair after falling down the cellar stairs as a child. Judge swapped Connemara for Tipperary because that was where his grandparents came from. By the end of the week the song had become the centrepiece of his act; he sold the publishing rights to Bert Feldman, who pepped it up with a brisk marching beat and credited both Judge and Williams as songwriters.

In August 1914, *Daily Mail* journalist George Curnock reported hearing a battalion of the Connaught Rangers (an Irish regiment based in Galway) singing the song to boost morale as they arrived in France. The paper printed its lyrics in full, ensuring that it became the biggest hit of the war. By November 1914 it had been recorded by popular Irish tenor John McCormack and later by the Australian star Florrie Forde. 'The song sold three million copies in the UK and six million worldwide after 1912,' Pybus told her local paper in 2014. 'Both men earned £164,000 between them in 1915 from royalties – a fortune at the time.'

As part of a 'simultaneous quodlibet' (songs whose complementary melodies mean you can sing them both at the same time), soldiers often combined it with 1915's 'Pack Up Your Your Troubles in Your Old Kit-Bag'. Both melodies were taken up and translated by the Germans in the opposite trenches. 'Tipperary' became a symbolic 'home' for frightened young men of all nationalities. As casualties mounted, the songs darkened and hardened with sexual innuendo and anti-officer sentiment. New arrivals attempting a bright 'Tipperary' were shouted down and taught the bawdier version: 'That's the wrong way to tickle Mary'.

The song appears in Joan Littlewood and the Theatre Workshop's 1963 establishment-rattling play (and, later, film), *Oh! What a Lovely War*, which marked the decade's shift towards an anti-war orthodoxy. The most haunting recent version was delivered by English folk singer June Tabor in 1999. She sings it as echoed 'back from the graveyards of Flanders' at the end of Bill Caddick's history lesson of a song, 'The Writing of Tipperary'.

Jack Judge lost his son to the war; some years later he sold

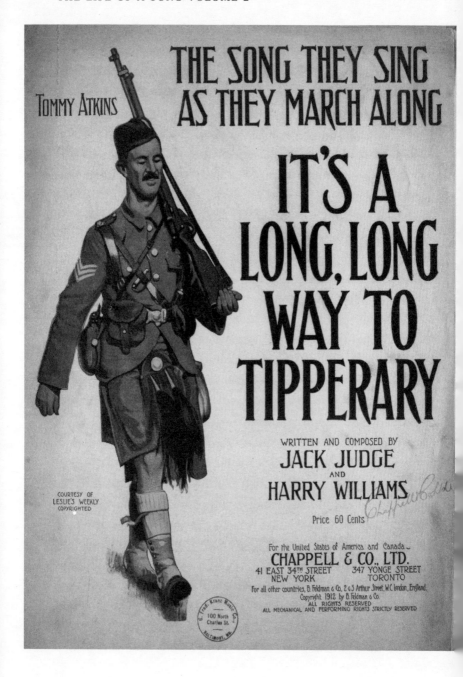

his copyright back to Williams for a fiver when he fell on hard times. Williams gave £1,000 (the equivalent of £65,000 today) to help the wounded, some of whom would have been shipped back to the barracks in Tipperary when it was converted to a military hospital.

Today the song is one of the oldest still bringing in royalties, which amount to around £30,000 a year for Williams's descendants, who include Pybus. In 2014 Pybus explained that: 'Although the copyright normally runs out after 70 years, because it's still performed in countries around the world, in films and even ringtones, we still own it.'

Meanwhile the people of Tipperary grew weary of being associated with war and set up their own peace prize. Nominees for the 2017 award included British–Lebanese human rights lawyer Amal Clooney and – more controversially – late Northern Ireland Deputy First Minister Martin McGuinness.

Helen Brown

33

GOLDEN SLUMBERS

Many Beatles tracks have had interesting afterlives, and 'Golden Slumbers' is one of them. It sits towards the end of the last album the band made together, 1969's *Abbey Road*, but it is less a song than a segment, a tender part of the medley at the end of side two. In one minute and 31 seconds, it evokes nostalgia, innocence and loss in its lyrics and melody, about the impossibility of getting back home ('Once there was a way...'), and the singing of lullabies to a child ('Sleep, pretty darling, do not cry'). In recent years, it has soundtracked prominent emotional moments in children's films, notably 2006's *Happy Feet* and 2016's *Sing*, and in 2017 it was covered by Elbow on the UK's biggest Christmas advert (for retail giant John Lewis). It also has its own fascinating, formative story.

On 2 July 1969, Paul McCartney was recording in Abbey Road without John Lennon, who had been in a car crash the previous day. So had Lennon's son Julian, his wife Yoko, and her daughter, Kyoko; all of them were in hospital in the Scottish Highlands, recovering from facial injuries or shock (three months later, Yoko would miscarry her and John's baby, their second loss in two years). Into this emotional mix came Paul McCartney. The previous October, he had been visiting his 62-year-old father Jim on the Wirral, in a house he had bought for him. One night, he was playing idly on the piano and found a music book belonging to his eight-year-old stepsister, Ruth. (Paul's beloved mother Mary died of cancer in 1956; his father married a young widow in 1964, and adopted her daughter.)

Lullabies were popular in sheet music in the early twentieth century, inspired by the success of Johannes Brahms' *Wiegenlied* and Chopin's Opus 57. McCartney came across a tune called 'Cradle Song'. 'I can't read music and I couldn't remember the old tune,' McCartney recalled in The Beatles' 1995 *Anthology* film. 'So I started just playing my tune to it . . . I liked the words so I kept that, and it fitted with another bit of song I had.' That other song was 'Carry That Weight', the next part of the *Abbey Road* medley, into which 'Golden Slumbers' neatly slides.

'Golden Slumbers' took its words from a song by the playwright Thomas Dekker which was couched in his 1603 play, *Patient Grissil*. This tells the story of Grissil, a poor basket-weaving woman courted and married by a wealthy marquess, who then subjects her to punishing psychological trials. One involves taking their baby away, but later the child is returned, the lullaby being sung to the baby by Grissil's father, Janiculo, to calm its cries. As he plays along on his lute, Janiculo's words run slightly differently to McCartney's. Golden slumbers 'kiss' the baby's eyes rather than 'fill' them. 'Pretty wantons' are urged not to cry, rather than a darling. The lines 'Once there was a way to get back homeward / Once there was a way to get back home' do not feature: these were McCartney's alone. Here was a man thinking about the comfort of families and homesteads as he sat by his father's piano, in the dying days of his band.

Sadness lurks in 'Golden Slumbers' from its beginning. A piano figure pivots between a chord that suggests a major key, before dropping in a mournful lower sixth. Unusually, the strings come in on this note, striking a strange, melancholy mood before its nursery-rhyme beauty lifts off.

The song's impact was instant: John Denver and Booker T & The MG's quickly covered it. Neil Diamond played it on tour. It has also become a touchstone for bands trying to show their sensitivity and maturity, with Mumford & Sons and Will Young recording it for radio sessions in the past decade. Its autumnal mood carries with it a knowledge of how time passes, which suits both the fabric of children's films and the development of artists' careers.

'Golden Slumbers' mourns those moments where we are looked after as children that we can never get back, before adulthood hits; then we have to 'carry that weight / a long time'. The year after he recorded 'Golden Slumbers', McCartney left The Beatles. He moved to south-west Scotland, to bring up his own children. He found a way to get back home.

Jude Rogers

34

9 TO 5

Dolly Parton was in her early thirties and teetering between stardom and the bargain bucket when Jane Fonda convinced her to take on her first acting role in *9 to 5*. She wrote the film's theme song on the back of a script, using her acrylic nails to tap out its typewriter rhythm, then roping in extras to layer vocals. With 22 albums already under her belt, the Nashville belle found Hollywood interminably slow.

In the 1980 workplace comedy-cum-social commentary *9 to 5*, Parton is Doralee Rhodes, a secretary whose sweet smile and abundant cleavage lead co-workers to presume she is having an affair with her much-reviled boss. They are wrong: Doralee is in fact a 'sleeper' deep behind enemy lines, a key player in the plot to kidnap her misogynistic manager.

The role must have hit a chord. Five feet tall and never seen without her blonde wigs and stage make-up, Parton knew what it meant to be pigeonholed. '9 to 5' was the moment she proved that classifications couldn't contain her. The song hit Number 1 on pop and country charts simultaneously, making Parton the first woman in more than two decades to do so and cementing her crossover appeal at a moment when country audiences were quick to condemn stars who courted the mainstream. *Rolling Stone* put her on the cover and called her 'unsinkable'.

'9 to 5' was also the closest that the famously apolitical Parton has ever come to activism. Concealed beneath a singalong melody, Parton's lyrics offer a sharp denunciation of how lives are squandered working for The Man, a message she drove home the following year when she performed the song at the Oscars in front of a backdrop featuring the slogan 'Unite'. No matter that the singer was herself living the American Dream, having shot from rural poverty to recording studios while still a child – '9 to 5' became an anthem for disgruntled office workers everywhere, and Parton America's unlikely every-woman.

In case anyone might accuse her of play-acting, Parton followed the single with *9 to 5 and Odd Jobs*, a concept album about work. It was as close to serious as Parton knew how to be, with covers including 'Deportee', Woody Guthrie's mournful ballad about migrant mortality. She picked her moment well. Ronald Reagan was sworn into office while the album was still riding high in the charts – a president who went on to disband unions and prioritize tax cuts for the wealthy.

'9 to 5' became a popular vehicle for parody and even had an audience with the president, when the satire group Capitol Steps performed it at the White House. '9 to 5' became 'Workin' 9 to 10', a ditty lampooning Reagan's supposedly lax work ethic.

More recent covers of '9 to 5' have pulled the song in one of two directions. There are the country singers who have sought to rework it as something more traditional: Alison Krauss had some critical success with a bluegrass version in 2003, and Home Free, the US's first all-vocal country band, released a cover on *Country Evolution* in 2015. Then there are the DJs for whom the song has provided bountiful raw material for dance remixes, sometimes entire albums' worth.

But Parton looms larger than life in the song's many itera-tions. She regularly duets with younger singers who cover it – a spotlight-savvy fairy godmother – and has started putting out her own dance remixes on reissues of the album. And when Patricia Resnick, the original screenwriter of 9 to 5, announced in 2006 that she was making the film into a musical, Parton turned her hand to show tunes and picked up a Tony Award nomination for Best Original Score.

In 2014, a 68-year-old Parton took to the Pyramid Stage at a particularly muddy edition of the Glastonbury Festival wearing a white rhinestone-covered cowgirl suit. '9 to 5' was the after-noon's most rousing singalong and, Parton said later, her biggest thrill. 'You did great,' she told the audience, the largest crowd that the festival had ever seen. 'I can't believe you know that song that well.' Then she sidestepped into a religious sermon. 'Amen,' bellowed the crowd, seemingly with conviction. Of all the audiences that Parton has converted, this was perhaps an easy sell: where better to perform this upbeat anti-work anthem than for a crowd who have escaped their 9 to 5 for one utopian weekend?

Harriet Fitch Little

TAKE FIVE

'Take Five', which in 1961 became the biggest jazz hit since the swing era, owes its existence to the US State Department. In 1956 some far-sighted official there launched the 'Jazz Ambassadors' programme, which aimed to promote American culture abroad (and allay concerns about racial tensions in the US) by sending musicians around the world. The ambassadors included Louis Armstrong, Duke Ellington, Dizzy Gillespie – and pianist Dave Brubeck, who was inspired to explore non-Western rhythms after hearing Bulgarian street musicians while on a State Department-sponsored visit to Turkey.

The result of Brubeck's eureka moment was *Time Out*, a 1959 album of music in unusual time-signatures such as 9/8, 6/4 and 5/4. It was a slow-burner, but two years after the album's release it spawned a hit single: 'Take Five'. Paul Desmond, the Dave Brubeck Quartet's alto saxophonist, had written 'Take Five' in order to showcase Joe Morello's drum solo – although in the event, a shorter version was released as a single with only a very brief drum solo (it had to be under three minutes in order to receive radio airplay). The Dave Brubeck Quartet were hugely popular due to assiduous touring of the college circuit, but were lambasted by jazz critics, who scorned them for an inability to swing and for their unadventurous improvisations. But with 'Take Five' they had pulled off an improbable coup. While it may have been an uncomplicated performance, with Brubeck playing piano chords throughout, it made listeners feel sophisticated. It allowed them to congratulate themselves for appreciating music in the 'difficult' time signature of 5/4.

. The song was picked up by musicians around the world, notably in Jamaica, where the most influential version was recorded in 1968 by Val Bennett; he changed the rhythm to a more danceable 4/4 and retitled it 'The Russians Are Coming' after Norman Jewison's then-popular film. Like many early reggae musicians, Bennett, a tenor saxophonist for Prince Buster, was a versatile player and well-versed in jazz – he had been a bandleader himself in the 1940s. 'The Russians Are Coming' inspired at least 50 further reggae covers, including a vocal arrangement by Horace Andy, a ska interpretation by Rico and a dub by King Tubby.

Did the appeal of 'Take Five' for a reggae audience lie in its mournful E-flat minor key, a common feature of the genre? Or perhaps it was the exotic origins of 'Take Five' that allowed it to transcend cultural boundaries. Whatever the case, the tune travels well. Stevie Wonder performed it as a harmonica solo; folk musician Davey Graham played it on acoustic guitar; Tito Puente arranged a mambo version for his Latin Ensemble; and singer Aziza Mustafa Zadeh recorded a scat incorporating Azerbaijani styles.

A particularly choice cut of 'Take Five' exotica is by Japanese musician Minoru Muraoka, who played the *shakuhachi*, a bamboo flutelike instrument. In 1970 he recorded an album called *Bamboo*, a fascinating attempt to fuse Japanese traditional styles with jazz and psychedelic rock. The opening track was his haunting version of 'Take Five', complete with drum solo. In 2011 a performance of 'Take Five' by a 60-piece ensemble of veteran Pakistani musicians that featured the sitar, sarod, tabla and dholak alongside Western instruments became a viral hit on YouTube.

Like Brubeck's original, the Sachal Studios Orchestra's 'Take Five' took a while to catch on. It had been recorded two years earlier in a labour of love by philanthropist Izzat Majeed, who became a life-long jazz aficionado as a boy after attending a Brubeck concert in Lahore in 1958. Realizing that American jazz and Pakistani ragas alike demanded improvisation, he built a studio in Lahore and assembled the veteran musicians, despite the risks of attack from Islamist extremists opposed to the West, and to music. The result was the subject of the documentary *Song of Lahore* and hailed as Pakistan's answer to Cuba's Buena Vista Social Club. And Brubeck, by this time 90 years old, acclaimed it as 'the most interesting and different recording of "Take Five" that I've heard'.

Jon Dennis

36

WALK ON THE WILD SIDE

Throughout the 1960s and 1970s the BBC was a notoriously squeamish organization, often banning records because of their 'offensive' content. In 1972, for instance, Paul McCartney's 'Hi, Hi, Hi' was removed from playlists because of its references to sex and drugs. In the same year, however, something much stronger slipped past the BBC's censors: Lou Reed's 'Walk on the Wild Side'. Despite references to male prostitution, transvestism, oral sex and drugs, the song was not blacklisted. These were innocent times, and perhaps the BBC's commissariat simply didn't understand what Reed was referring to when he sang (albeit in a mumbly delivery) about 'giving head' (though the line was cut for the US release).

The song was a worldwide hit (helped by the fact that 'Perfect Day' was on the B-side) and the subsequent album *Transformer* transformed Reed's profile, leading to a resurgence of interest in his old band The Velvet Underground, and in their patron Andy Warhol and his Factory. 'Walk on the Wild Side' is Reed's memoir of his years at the Factory, with its cast of characters from Warhol's 'superstars' who appeared in his films, *Flesh* (1968), *Trash* (1970) and *Heat* (1972). 'Candy', for instance, was transgender actress Candy Darling, who had made an earlier appearance in Reed's Velvet Underground song 'Candy Says' ('Candy says . . . I've come to hate my body'). 'Little Joe' was

Joe Dallesandro, the athletic, oft-naked star of Warhol's *Flesh*. The 'Sugar Plum Fairy' was an amalgamation of characters who were essentially drug delivery men.

Before *Transfomer*, Reed had been at a low ebb. He had left The Velvet Underground in 1970 and released a solo album (featuring Rick Wakeman on keyboards) which sold poorly. Meanwhile in 1972, David Bowie's career was taking off and everything he touched seemed to turn to platinum. Bowie had long been an admirer of The Velvet Underground – he played their song 'White Light/White Heat' in his shows, and had referenced them on the sleeve notes to his *Hunky Dory* album. Bowie and his guitarist Mick Ronson were hired to produce Reed's *Transformer* at Trident Studios in London.

The session for 'Walk on the Wild Side' began at 10am on a Monday, and among the musicians was veteran session bassist Herbie Flowers (also, incidentally, the co-writer of Clive Dunn's 1970 novelty hit 'Grandad'). Flowers came from a jazz background and was accustomed to improvising; he came up with the unforgettable bassline on his double bass, then overdubbed it on his Fender fretless electric 10 notes higher to achieve the sweet, slinky sound, accentuated by the way the two basslines move in opposite directions. The session fee was £12 but Flowers got £17 because of the overdub. It took about 20 minutes.

These days no musician would talk about 'coloured girls' ('And the coloured girls go . . . ') but in 1972 this was acceptable parlance. Curiously, however, the three singers who provided the backing vocals were three white English women who went under the name of the Thunderthighs; the following year they sang 'Sha-na-na-na-push-push' on Mott the Hoople's hit, 'Roll Away the Stone'.

'Walk on the Wild Side' has been covered or sampled by a

handful of artists. In 2012 the British–Canadian collective the Flowers of Hell released an atmospheric version which, intriguingly, featured Reed's earlier – and less lubricious – lyrics from a demo recording. In 2014 the funk-metal-rap band Tackhead recorded a muscular rendition. Most famously, it was sampled in 1991 by A Tribe Called Quest; their track 'Can I Kick It?' casts the bassline in a deliciously slinky groove over which they deliver a rap that, with lines such as 'Come and spread your arms if you really need a hug', can, in rap terms, be best described as a Walk on the Mild Side.

David Cheal

37

ME AND MRS JONES

Fornication and adultery were illegal in Pennsylvania until 1973. Laws prohibiting them were abolished that year, but not without a struggle. In November 1972, as the new criminal code was being debated, a Democrat in the state legislature proposed an amendment protecting the ban. It was defeated by 111 votes to 73.

The blow to Pennsylvanian morality came three nights after Philadelphian singer Billy Paul appeared on the television show *Soul Train*. He wore a suave velvet suit and sang his new single, 'Me and Mrs Jones', as couples slow-danced around the foot of the stage. The song was about adultery.

'Me and Mrs Jones, we got a thing going on,' Paul sang in a beautifully sultry tone. 'We both know that it's wrong, but it's much too strong to let it go now.' Tinkling piano, strings and a sighing saxophone made the extramarital liaison sound the very height of sophistication. Never has the seventh commandment been broken so smoothly.

The song, which went on to hit Number 1 in the US, was written by Kenny Gamble, Leon Huff and lyricist Cary Gilbert. Gamble and Huff (good names for a production duo) were instrumental in creating Philadelphia soul, a lushly orchestral style that supplanted Motown in the 1970s. They were inspired to write 'Me and Mrs Jones' by the sight of a couple who

regularly met in the bar below their office, always playing the same song on the jukebox. Perhaps that song was Doris Day's 'Secret Love', from the 1953 film *Calamity Jane*. The melody of the first line Day sings, 'Once I had a secret love', is slyly quoted by the sax solo at the start of 'Me and Mrs Jones'.

I doubt that the 73 legislators who voted to keep Pennsylvania's anti-adultery laws were *Soul Train* viewers. But it is tempting to imagine them watching Paul sing 'Me and Mrs Jones' with mounting outrage, and perhaps an intuition of defeat. It is a supremely worldly song, knowing and seductive, aware of the misdeed it describes and the impossibility of legislating against it.

'Me and Mrs Jones' has been covered numerous times. The fate is apt. Cover versions are music's version of adultery, a coveting of thy neighbour's song. The best ones are caught between fidelity and faithlessness. They must be true to the song being covered while also taking the liberty of adding something: otherwise the result is karaoke. A degree of adulteration is vital.

Of the many interpretations of 'Me and Mrs Jones', the most memorable is also the most faithless. It is Amy Winehouse's 'Me and Mr Jones', from her 2006 album *Back to Black*. Winehouse's version swaps the original's rich soul for louche doo-wop and alters Mrs Jones's gender. The lyrics are addressed to a nameless man with whom the singer is having an on-off relationship. To her annoyance he has made her miss a show by the rapper Slick Rick. She is determined that he won't allow her to miss a show by a New York rapper she loves even more, Nas (real name Nasir Jones).

The cheating runs both ways. 'Can't believe you played me out like that,' Winehouse tells the nameless lover. But in the next breath she pledges herself to Nas ('Nobody stands in-between me and my man / Cause it's me and Mr Jones'). Her voice is slurred, vivacious; she follows her own tune as though two-timing the jaunty doo-wop. What a wonderful singer she was, and how awful that the one thing she couldn't cheat was death.

Ludovic Hunter-Tilney

38

I WISH I KNEW HOW IT WOULD FEEL TO BE FREE

To generations of British TV viewers, its full-octave, syncopated piano chords and grooving bass are instantly recognizable as the theme tune to the BBC's *Film* review series. But to Americans, 'I Wish I Knew How It Would Feel to Be Free' has deeper resonances, being best known as a civil rights anthem. When Nina Simone recorded it on her 1967 album *Silk and Soul*, almost instantly it became a freedom song, up there with 'A Change is Gonna Come' and 'Blowin' in the Wind'.

Yet this irresistibly catchy 16-bar gospel-jazz tune began life as an instrumental. Born in 1921 in North Carolina, composer Billy Taylor was a gifted pianist who had built an impressive jazz pedigree working in New York with bebop luminaries such as Dizzy Gillespie, Artie Shaw and Charlie Parker. By the 1960s, he was also a broadcaster and civil rights campaigner, and had recorded many albums, mostly with his trio. Bucking that trend, the first recording of 'I Wish I Knew' on Taylor's 1963 album *Right Here, Right Now* had a big-band line-up of 19 musicians. With Ben Tucker on bass and Grady Tate on drums, Taylor's eloquent piano solo is bookended by a full horn chorus that's almost hymnal. (The version used by the BBC was recorded later, with a trio, in 1967.)

But the song had yet to be performed or recorded with lyrics. Billy Taylor's daughter Kim Taylor-Thompson, a law professor in New York, had initially spurred her father to write the song when she came home from school singing a spiritual. Kim takes up the story (via email) of how it acquired lyrics. 'Dad initially recorded it as an instrumental. But, as I recall, he had written the first verse of the lyrics pretty early on. He got stuck at one point and invited [lyricist] Dick Dallas to collaborate to help him finish the lyrics and that's when we got the later verses. I've always felt that there was a difference between the first verse and the later ones. I think you hear my dad's voice most clearly in the first verse.'

So, as soon as Nina Simone sang, 'I wish I could break all the chains holding me' on *Silk and Soul*, the floodgates were open. Simone's artistry and passion took the song to another level, one that resonated not only with the civil rights movement but with issues of identity and individualism. Like Taylor, Simone was born in North Carolina, and church music played a large part in her childhood; like him she had a formal musical training; like him she was an activist, and in her impassioned treatment of the song on *Silk and Soul* her voice is clear, sincere, without irony.

Subsequent versions of the song were less convincing. The following year, the song reached Number 68 in the US charts in a recording by Solomon Burke that begins with the cheesy voiceover: 'Have you ever wished upon a star / And all your hopes seem so far?' Folk singers John Denver and Mary Travers produced earnest guitar-strumming versions. In 2001, UK duo Lighthouse Family released a wistfully yearning version featuring the mellifluous voice of Tunde Baiyewu. Emeli Sandé's 2013 rendition is full of soulful intent.

Meanwhile Coca-Cola capitalized on the song's feelgood factor with a 2004 TV advert featuring British singer Sharlene

Hector, though the lyrics were changed to the schmaltzy 'I wish I could share all the love that's in my heart', with Hector strolling down a US street handing out bottles of Coke to delighted passers-by.

All of which is a world away from the gutsy Simone. It was in live concerts that she really took possession of the song, giving it a powerful, personal rawness. Like a gospel preacher, she improvised with the lyrics, turning their message of hope into positive affirmation: 'I know how it feels / Not to be chained / to any race / to any face'. At the Montreux Jazz Festival in 1976 she put on a storming show, transporting the audience while simultaneously showing her effortless mastery of piano styles from swing to baroque. Above all, Simone gave herself completely to the freedom of performance, of being herself, doing and saying exactly as she felt at the time. In the film *Nina* directed by Joel Gold, she said that freedom for her meant 'no fear'. Her fearlessness is the legacy of the song.

Alison Gunn

39

NO SCRUBS

One of the biggest records of 1999 was, simply, a complaint about inadequate men. 'No Scrubs' by TLC was the second-biggest selling single of 1999 in the US, behind Cher's 'Believe', and sold a total of 677,000 copies in the UK, peaking at Number 3. Emerging at the height of a phase of staggering invention in US R&B, when producers such as Timbaland and Rodney Jerkins were deploying technology to create a new, coldly synthetic style, it wielded an influence out of proportion even to its massive sales. In Texas, for example, a young female vocal group was paying close attention: 'TLC has influenced just about every female group that's out there now, and they definitely influenced Destiny's Child,' said a young Beyoncé Knowles, the leader of Destiny's Child, who quickly adopted the defiant stance of 'No Scrubs' and found themselves eclipsing their idols.

'No Scrubs' had been written by Kevin 'She'kspere' Briggs, a producer at TLC's label LaFace, but was transformed when Tameka Cottle and Kandi Burruss heard his version and asked to rewrite the lyrics. 'She had a concept 'cause she had been, like, "I wanna talk about a screw-up, a guy that's a screw-up that doesn't have their own business in order",' Cottle told *Rolling Stone* of Burruss's idea. 'It came from a previous relationship that she was in.'

'Scrub' was a piece of Atlanta slang, but the song had to

define it, which Cottle and Burruss did with the chorus, offering no sympathy for the subject: 'A scrub is a guy that can't get no love from me / Hanging out the passenger side / Of his best friend's ride / Trying to holler at me.'

Cottle and Burruss had recently left the R&B group Xscape and were trying to forge a career as a duo. 'No Scrubs' was to be their breakout hit. Until it wasn't. Recognizing the strength of the song, Briggs took it to the executives at LaFace, who reassigned it to TLC, a far greater priority for them. Burruss and Cottle weren't too disheartened – the publishing royalties from a hit of the magnitude of 'No Scrubs' were immense, the song won them Grammy awards, and opened the door to a songwriting career for Burruss.

'No Scrubs' was a perfect package. The lyric was memorable, while Briggs' arrangement – centred on a Spanish-flavoured acoustic guitar, electronic percussion and the breathy samples that were the trick *du jour* of late-90s R&B – was both gossamer light and rhythmically sturdy. And TLC were the perfect trio to deliver it, a girl group who did not need to shout slogans about 'girl power', but who seemed genuinely willing to take on men they didn't care for, physically if necessary (in 1994, Lisa 'Left Eye' Lopes set fire to a pair of shoes belonging to her abusive boyfriend and as a result burnt down the mansion they shared).

It didn't take long for 'No Scrubs' to enter the public consciousness. Within months, the male hip-hop group Sporty Thievz had answered with 'No Pigeons', repurposing the backing track to defend the honour of feckless men against snooty women. And the cover versions followed: Scout Niblett turned 'No Scrubs' into spectral, mournful Americana; Bastille did their big, emotive pop thing with it; it turned up on the *Glee*

soundtrack. And then it became an element of the biggest song of 2017 – the most streamed song ever on Spotify – when Ed Sheeran's 'Shape of You' gave a songwriting credit to Cottle, Burruss and She'kspere.

Eighteen years later, 'No Scrubs' still sounds like a record from pop's future. And still, when it is played by DJs, you can see women take to the dance floor in groups and sing to each other: "Cause I'm looking like class, and he's looking like trash / Can't get wit' a deadbeat ass.' And you can see the men shrink a little.

Michael Hann

40

NATURE BOY

The Brooklyn-born musician who wrote Nat King Cole's 1948 hit 'Nature Boy' certainly embodied its title. By the time he composed this soft, mystic song, he was living in woods and parks around Los Angeles, playing piano in a raw food restaurant. He had also changed his name to eden ahbez, insisting on a lower case spelling on the grounds that 'only God and Infinity deserve capitals'.

The song mixes autobiography with spiritual convictions. The 'strange, enchanted boy' of the opening stanza is surely ahbez, and its climax – 'The greatest thing you'll ever learn, is just to love and be loved in return' – is a moral imperative. Yet this gentle song's early trajectory included a strike, legal action and racial bigotry.

ahbez was part of a back-to-nature movement whose followers were known as the Nature Boys. They were influenced by earlier European *Naturmensch* and *Lebensreform* philosophies, but this was the US of the 1940s and ahbez was just considered weird. 'I look crazy, but I'm not,' he told *Life* magazine in 1948. 'And the funny thing is that other people don't look crazy, but they are.'

When ahbez tried to present the manuscript to Cole, he was rebuffed. But a crumpled manuscript did eventually reach the singer, reputedly slipped to his valet. Cole immediately included it in his trio's repertoire but needed ahbez's permission for recording. He was found camping with his wife and child below one of the 'L's of the Hollywood sign.

Cole recorded 'Nature Boy' for Capitol in August 1947 but the label thought the song wayward and shelved it. It was released only because the American Federation of Musicians entered into a lengthy dispute, banning all instrumental recording, so that labels were forced to draw on work that was already in the bag. Cole's shelved version of 'Nature Boy' got its turn in March 1948 and chalked up 1 million sales, establishing Cole's solo career.

It also made an unlikely celebrity of ahbez, who, interviewed in 1948 on Chicago radio show *We the People*, pronounced: 'I was born with a love of nature and I was born with the desire to find God.'

But trouble was in the offing. The composer and Yiddish theatre star Herman Yablokoff accused ahbez of appropriating 'Nature Boy' from his own song 'Shvayg Mayn Harts' ('Be Still My Heart'); ahbez, though insisting that the tune had come to him in the California mountains, settled out of court.

Cole, meanwhile, had to wear skin-lightening make-up to perform the song on television, and burning crosses were erected outside his new home in a white LA neighbourhood. Yet his version of 'Nature Boy' was a bridgehead across a racially divided US – something later versions recognized. Included in this strand is the orchestral version that leads off Marvin Gaye's 1965 Nat King Cole tribute album, and George Benson's slinky, soulful version on the 1977 album *In Flight*.

Others chose 'Nature Boy' for its commercial appeal. Frank Sinatra had an early hit with choral backing; rock'n'roll crooner Bobby Darin charted with it in 1961, and British soul-funk band

Central Line performed it on the BBC's *Top of the Pops* in 1983. A David Bowie version is included on the soundtrack of the 2001 film *Moulin Rouge!*

A separate strand drew on the song's spiritual message. Saxophonist John Coltrane turned it into an instrumental lament on the 1965 album *The John Coltrane Quartet Plays*; in the same year, Grace Slick's rough and ready reading brought it to the attention of the counterculture. In comparison, Sun Ra's off-kilter account on the 1977 album *Some Blues But Not the Kind That's Blue* is almost tranquil.

Interest in ahbez was rekindled when Lady Gaga and Tony Bennett included 'Nature Boy' on their 2014 collaboration *Cheek to Cheek*. 'This composer was part of a subculture of nomadic hippies!' Lady Gaga tweeted. 'We channelled our own Gypsy lives in this performance.'

You do have to wonder what the vegetarian ahbez would have made of Gaga's meat dress.

Mike Hobart

TEARDROP

In 2017 a doctoral student at Ohio State University discovered that song intros are on average 78 per cent shorter today than they were 30 years ago. In the age of streaming, we have become impatient with our music, skipping from one track to the next without stopping to luxuriate in a song. Our demand for immediacy means that labels now require artists to get to the chorus – the real selling point – as quickly as possible.

When Massive Attack released 'Teardrop' as a single from their 1998 album *Mezzanine*, this climate of musical efficiency had not yet taken hold. With an intro that builds for more than a minute, it's hard to imagine that a song so spare and sombre would be made today. For 62 seconds before the first word, the pioneers of trip-hop (an emergent genre in the 1990s) add layer upon layer of sound to create a richly textured, immersive track.

The song was initially built around the heartbeat-like rhythm of the bass drum – a sample of a little-known jazz piece by Les McCann from 1973 called 'Sometimes I Cry' – which lends the track its keen sense of vitality, and the indelible 'modern Baroque' harpsichord riff. The group recorded an instrumental demo in April 1997 and set about finding the right singer to suit the ethereal melody.

In the end it came down to a choice between Madonna and

a singer described by some critics as possessing 'the voice of God' – Elizabeth Fraser of the Cocteau Twins. Fearing that Madonna would take the song too much into pop territory, band members Robert Del Naja and Grantley Marshall outvoted Andrew Vowles in favour of Fraser's crystalline vocals.

Fraser was in an appropriately mournful state of mind when she recorded the song. The words, though esoteric almost to the point of incomprehension, are imbued with melancholy, born from Fraser's own sadness on learning about the death of her friend Jeff Buckley in May 1997. '["Teardrop" is] kind of about him – that's how it feels to me anyway,' she said in 2009. The song seems a fitting tribute to Buckley, whose own music is similarly sorrowful and otherworldly. 'Teardrop' went on to reach the dizzy heights of the UK Top 10 in 1998.

In the two decades since 'Teardrop' was first released, there have been more than 20 cover versions. In the mid-2000s, the medical drama *House* adopted the track as its title credits theme, giving it a new lease of life.

Two of the best covers, both by superbly dexterous guitarists, Newton Faulkner and José González, came out in 2007. Faulkner does away with the lengthy introduction, but recreates the heartbeat rhythm in the idiosyncratic way he plays his guitar percussively between notes. González's version is more stripped back, taking on the original's complex layering with a single guitar. The famously reticent Swedish–Argentine songwriter brings a vulnerability to the song; his accented voice means that we focus less on decoding the lyrics and more on the emotions elicited.

A cover by English soft-rockers Elbow was included on their 2006 *B-Sides and Remixes* album. Theirs is a largely faithful

rendition in terms of tone and pacing, but the avuncular gruff-
ness of Guy Garvey's voice reinvents the song as a warm, homey
tune, bereft of the eerie beauty evoked by Fraser.

Conversely, Scottish rock band Simple Minds amplify the
song's uncanniness. Jim Kerr's vocal performance verges on the
sinister, while a combination of throbbing electronica and a
series of atonal sound effects creates an intriguingly spooky
composition.

In 2011, Gary Barlow amassed a group of young Brits
including Ed Sheeran and Tinchy Stryder to record a single for
the Children in Need charity appeal. Though titled 'Teardrop',
the song only samples Massive Attack, instead featuring new
lyrics relevant to the cause. Although no one can fault the

collective's intentions, the cover is marred by overdone production and po-faced performances.

In truth, no recording has recreated the haunting atmosphere
of Massive Attack's 1998 classic. And few mainstream musicians
today would be afforded the freedom to release such a slow-
burning track.

Dan Einav

42

STRANGE FRUIT

Late in 2016, the British singer and one-time *X Factor* runner-up Rebecca Ferguson received an invitation to perform at the inauguration ceremony of President Donald Trump. It would be the most high-profile performance of her career, following in the footsteps of Aretha Franklin and Kelly Clarkson, who sang at the inaugurations of Barack Obama.

Ferguson replied that she would be delighted to accept on condition that she could perform 'Strange Fruit'. Made famous by Billie Holiday, the song, she explained, 'was blacklisted in the United States for being too controversial. A song that speaks to all the disregarded and downtrodden black people in the United States. A song that is a reminder of how love is the only thing that will conquer all the hatred in this world.' Ferguson never heard back from Trump's people and ended up watching the ceremony on TV.

Before it was a song, 'Strange Fruit' was a poem, written by Abel Meeropol, a Jewish high school teacher from the Bronx. He was inspired by a now well-known photograph of two black teenagers who were lynched in the town of Marion, Indiana, in 1930. A mob broke into the jail where they were being held for allegedly murdering a white factory worker and raping his female companion. They dragged the boys outside, killed them and hung them from a tree for all to see.

Set in the rustic loveliness of the 'gallant South', Meeropol's poem provided an unflinching description of a 'black body swinging in the southern breeze' with 'the bulging eyes and the twisted mouth', and where the scent of magnolia is supplanted by the stench of burning flesh. It first appeared in 1937 under the title 'Bitter Fruit' in the union publication *The New York Teacher*. Later Meeropol set it to music and played it to the owner of the Greenwich Village cabaret club Café Society, who passed it on to Billie Holiday, one of the club's regular performers. Early in 1939, she sang it while standing under a single spotlight in front of a shocked crowd. Holiday later recalled that at first 'there wasn't even a patter of applause. Then a lone person began to clap nervously. Then suddenly everyone was clapping.'

Holiday asked her label, Columbia, to record it but, fearing a backlash, it declined. She went to Commodore Records and, accompanied by her eight-piece Café Society band, recorded it in a single afternoon. 'Strange Fruit' would become her biggest hit and signature track, and would be described by the jazz writer Leonard Feather as 'the first significant protest in words and music, the first unmuted cry against racism'. The record producer and co-founder of Atlantic Records, Ahmet Ertegun, called it 'a declaration of war . . . the beginning of the civil rights movement'. Performing the song was banned in some US cities for fear of provoking civil unrest.

Holiday's 'Strange Fruit' has long been viewed as the definitive version, dripping as it is with pain and disgust, although Nina Simone came close with her similarly bleak 1965 version. She once described it as 'the ugliest song I have ever heard. Ugly in the sense that it is violent and tears at the guts of what white people have done to my people in this country.' Other interpreters have included Diana Ross, Jeff Buckley, Siouxsie and the Banshees, Cocteau Twins and Robert Wyatt. Most recently, Kanye West revived interest in the song when he sampled Simone's recording for his 2013 track 'Blood on the Leaves'.

In 1999 *Time* magazine called Holiday's version the song of the century, though that doesn't mean that the world has grown comfortable with its ferocious imagery and malignant tone. Eighty years after it was written, this powerful portrait of racial violence still has the capacity to break hearts and stun audiences.

Fiona Sturges

43

O SOLE MIO

A Neapolitan ballad, 'O Sole Mio' has enjoyed more than one life. Its lilting melody has been reincarnated and renamed several times since it first appeared in 1898. 'O Sole Mio' ('My Sunshine') was composed by Eduardo Di Capua. Its lyric, comparing a lover's face with the sun, was written by a poet, Giovanni Capurro. In 1916 the celebrated tenor Enrico Caruso recorded it for a 78rpm single on the Victor label, a version that has been repackaged more than 90 times. Mario Lanza was another celebrity tenor to pick up the song, recording it in 1950.

But there was more to 'O Sole Mio' than a list of acclaimed operatic recordings. In 1915, it was given its first English trans-lation by Charles W Harrison, an American tenor, and in 1921 its melody was adapted into a popular hymn, 'Down From His Glory'. A year earlier, 'O Sole Mio' had become a surrogate national anthem at the Antwerp Olympics when the music for the Italian anthem was mislaid.

Tony Martin, an American crooner and actor, enjoyed a hit single with an English-language version called 'There's No Tomorrow' in 1950. Eight years later, Martin was attending a cabaret event for showbusiness figures in Hollywood when one of the comedians, Harry Einstein, suffered a heart attack on stage. In a grim scene, a surgeon in the house operated on the victim using a penknife, while another used bare electric wires as a defibrillator. In the spirit of 'the show must go on', Martin was called to the stage to sing 'There's No Tomorrow'. For the unfortunate Einstein, it proved true: he died that night.

Elvis Presley loved Martin's record. He taped his own version in 1959 while stationed in Germany with the US Army, a performance that went unreleased until 1997. Presley also asked his music publisher to create a new song around the melody, who gave the job to composers Aaron Schroeder and Wally Gold. It took them two hours to complete the lyrics for 'It's Now or Never', and Presley's sensitive and elegant 1960 recording became the second biggest-selling single of his career.

Reggae vocalist Jimmy London covered it in 1972, one of several Presley hits he tackled. Country singer John Schneider chose the song for his debut single in 1981. Paul McCartney paid homage to it in 1990 on *The Last Temptation of Elvis*, an album made for the music magazine *NME*.

'O Sole Mio' was not finished, however. Elvis often explained the origins of 'It's Now or Never' on stage, and his 1977 album *Elvis In Concert* (released six weeks after Elvis's death) featured the tenor Sherrill Nielsen singing it before Elvis delivered his own hit version. 'O Sole Mio' earned Pavarotti a Grammy Award for Best Classical Vocal Solo in 1980, and there was even a formulaic electronic house mix, credited to Operatix, in 1992, which sampled Caruso's 1916 version.

The song won fresh fame in the 1980s when it was used to advertise ice cream in a UK TV campaign that ran (or dribbled) for a decade. The lyrics ('Just one Cornetto, give it to me . . .') were supposedly sung by the Italian-born, Sutton Coldfield-resident tenor Renato Pagliari, who had a hit with 'Save Your Love' in 1982 as half of the novelty pop act Renée & Renato. After Renato died, his son revealed that he had not actually sung on the commercial. Whoever was responsible, it kept the ditty in the public consciousness and certainly prompted the football chant: 'Just one Capello, give him to me, delicious manager, from Italy,' sung about the England manager Fabio Capello in 2008. The melody had another period of popularity in the UK when Elvis's version made Number 1 again in 2005. 'It's Now or Never'? 'It's Now and Forever' would be more accurate.

Ian McCann

44

SUMMERTIME

In 1935, George and Ira Gershwin and the author DuBose
Heyward premiered their folk opera *Porgy and Bess*. It was not,
initially, a success. But many of its songs swiftly became stand-
ards: 'I Got Plenty O' Nuttin'', 'I Loves You, Porgy', 'It Ain't
Necessarily So'. And above all, possibly the most recorded song
ever, 'Summertime'.

Many of the opera's lyrics were by Ira Gershwin: you can
hear his love of wordplay when 'It Ain't Necessarily So' rhymes
'things that you're liable' with 'to read in the Bible'. But
'Summertime' was by DuBose Heyward, on whose novel, *Porgy*,
the opera was based. No wordplay here, no puns or ingenious
rhymes. 'Summertime', sings Clara the fisherman's wife – and
any number of singers after her, that last syllable stretched out
languorously – 'and the livin' is easy'. But the backing swells
like a thunderhead. Your father may be rich and your mother
good-looking, but this is a temporary idyll: 'One of these morn-
ings / you're going to rise up singing / Then you'll spread your
wings and you'll take to the sky . . .'. Summer, in other words,
is a transitory premonition of an eternal heaven.

This tension between a hard life on earth and rewards in
the hereafter is a trope that starts with the spiritual – which
'Summertime', in formal terms, is – but in other songs is rejected.
In 'Ol' Man River' the chorus are 'tired of livin' / but scared of

dyin' ', and for Sam Cooke, in 1964's 'A Change Is Gonna Come', 'It's been too hard living, but I'm afraid to die / 'Cause I don't know what's up there, beyond the sky.' In 'Summertime', hedonism and eschatology are in perfect equipoise.

Gershwin insisted that *Porgy and Bess* should be performed by a black cast – which posed some problems for the New York debut when he turned down Al Jolson, and failed to land Paul Robeson. The all-black cast can still carry immense symbolic power, as in 1997 at the State Theatre in Pretoria, when a mix of South African and American singers brought the opera to the heart of the Afrikaner establishment.

The song, however, has long since broken free from the opera. There have been instrumentals: recordings by Sidney Bechet on clarinet, in 1938, and Miles Davis on trumpet, 20 years later, are as well-known as any of the sung versions. There have been untold numbers of jazz renditions, among which Billie Holiday and Ella Fitzgerald stand out. There have been rock interpretations: Janis Joplin's 1968 recording starts out baroque and ends up belting the blues; The Doors interpolated 'Summertime' into live versions of 'Light My Fire'.

On any portmanteau re-recording of Gershwin's songs, 'Summertime' is the prize. Peter Gabriel – who rarely records cover versions – contributed a version in 1994. It opens with an extended harmonica voluntary from Larry Adler, and then Gabriel sings more in weary resignation than sunstruck languor. Gabriel's summer sounds as arduous as the trudged roads of his own 'Don't Give Up'.

On a charity compilation a few years later, the song went to the acceptable face of trip-hop, the band Morcheeba. The music shimmers in the heat. The veteran American flautist Hubert Laws coils tendrils of flute around the melody, while Skye

Edwards sings less as if trying to soothe a baby to sleep than as if she herself has only just awoken, and is stretching into a new day. Slyly, for the last reprise, she switches which parent is rich and which good-looking.

Perhaps the song's popularity in its home country recognizes the fragility of the American summer. In a country where even today the average annual vacation entitlement is three weeks, and only a quarter of workers take their full entitlement (one in seven takes no holiday at all), the idea of the livin' being easy sounds like a fantasy. Those rich daddies come at a high price.

David Honigmann

45

A WHITER SHADE
OF PALE

How long is the life of a song? In such an ephemeral art form as popular music, a year can seem a long time. We are just getting our heads around the idea that songs that were meant to last in the public consciousness for a few weeks are actually tumbling from one zeitgeist to another over the course of several decades.

But sometimes there is a longer narrative at play: a piece of music written centuries ago can suddenly re-emerge in a quite different guise. But can we even recognize it?

Procol Harum's 'A Whiter Shade of Pale', released in May 1967, was a song that was both of and against its time. Its druggy tempo and artful lyrics chimed perfectly with the air of cultural experimentation of the 1960s. Its apparently nonsensical opening line – 'We skipped the light fandango' – has inspired laboured analysis, sourced, by some, in the writings of Milton and Shakespeare. But the melancholy tenor of the song's melody was, as the parlance of the time would have it, a downer.

'A Whiter Shade of Pale', attributed at the time to Gary Brooker and Keith Reid, tried to scupper the Summer of Love before it even got properly started. The lyric, said Reid many years later, told the story of a seduction. But its eroticism was imbued with sadness. Reid had been watching those desperate masterpieces of European art house cinema, *Pierrot le Fou* and *Last Year at Marienbad*. The song's three short verses were similarly joyless and alienating: 'I was feeling kinda seasick / But the crowd called out for more'.

As for the melody, it seemed to belong to a different time altogether. Which it did. The more sophisticated commentators of the time could not help but point out similarities between the song and the sublime baroque music of Bach. Brooker did not deny it. He had listened to 'Air on a G String', he said, and it set off a 'spark' within him, contributing to the lugubrious chord progression of his hit song.

'A Whiter Shade of Pale' reached the top of the charts all over the world. It was an undeniably classy piece of work, and by the time the Summer of Love had ended, its downbeat flavour was recognized as prescient. It settled into the national treasure category of favourite hit singles, became covered in more than 700 versions (none memorable), and was heard in just about every meaningful film about the 1960s.

But nearly 40 years after its release, the issue of that musical dialogue between Bach and Brooker was raised again. This time it was the group's organist Matthew Fisher who brought it up. Fisher went to court to claim a share in the song's royalties. It was he who was at least partly responsible for the song's melody, he argued. Intriguingly, Fisher too admitted a debt to Bach. Yes, the song did sound like a piece of his music. But it was not 'Air on a G String'. Fisher claimed he based the melody on Bach's 'Sleepers, Awake' cantata, which he mashed up with The Teddy Bears' hit 'To Know Him Is to Love Him'. Brooker, by contrast, claimed he had been inspired by another cross-fertilization: the bars of the composer's music used in the famous Hamlet cigar advertisement.

In 2009, the House of Lords ruled in Fisher's favour, and decreed that he should share in future royalties from the song. It concluded a case which had been a fascinating exercise in how something so malleable as a melody can survive in the collective subconscious for hundreds of years. Has any Number 1 single claimed such a rich and complicated heritage? Is there a longer life of a pop song than this?

Peter Aspden

46

I'VE GOT YOU UNDER MY SKIN

Here's a question for you. In which musical did 'I've Got You Under My Skin' first appear, and by whom was it sung? Award yourself ten points and a pat on the back if you answered *Born to Dance* ('MGM's dazzling successor to *Great Ziegfeld!*') and Virginia Bruce (who serenaded a startlingly young James Stewart).

As soon as *Born to Dance* was released, other musicians recognized the brilliance of the composition: of Cole Porter's swooping, lovesick melody, his elegant, wry lyrics. Lee Wiley sounded even more heartbroken than Bruce; Al Bowlly – in some respects a precursor to Sinatra, in that he introduced the idea of the singer as the star, rather than the bandleader – fronted a busily and bizarrely Latin version for the Ray Noble orchestra. There were other recordings in those first months after the film, from Carroll Gibbons and others, but it was another 20 years before the song took on the identity it has held ever since.

Frank Sinatra's career revival was well under way by the time he entered Capitol Studios in Los Angeles in early 1956 to record *Songs for Swingin' Lovers!*. His three albums since signing to Capitol had all been Top 5 hits, but *Songs for Swingin' Lovers!*, his fourth, was something else: a record that defined, variously, an artist, an aesthetic, a lifestyle and an era. To this day, when some young male singer wants to capture the essence of 1950s showbiz glamour, it is to *Songs for Swingin' Lovers!* he turns.

The album's centrepiece was 'I've Got You Under My Skin', carefully sequenced to stand out between the more easy-going 'Love Is Here to Stay' and 'I Thought About You'. The intro is almost tinkling, a light shuffle, Sinatra sounding at his most relaxed. Then, at 2'15", the song is transformed: the orchestra has been vamping up and Milt Bernhart's trombone solo – written hurriedly, but delivered perfectly – unleashes a frenzy. Suddenly, the song is about not pent-up desire but unleashed desire. When Sinatra returns he's no longer gentle, he's insistent. The recording is a triumph, for Sinatra, Bernhart and for arranger Nelson Riddle and producer Voyle Gilmore.

Sinatra's version is so definitive that it overshadows all other big-band arrangements. Ella Fitzgerald's version, from the same year, sounds like a tea party in comparison. The recent trend for 'American songbook' albums by pop artists has done neither the artists nor the song any favours: Rod Stewart's version, with synths over a string section, is horrible. Peter Andre's is a direct copy of the Sinatra arrangement in the same way someone making an Airfix model is directly copying a Spitfire. Carly Simon's is pleasant, but pointless. Cliff Richard, as ever, sounds like a man reading aloud about love from a Haynes car maintenance manual.

Best are the instrumental recordings (Oscar Peterson, Charlie Parker), and those where the artist has taken the song some-where else entirely. In 1966, Bob Gaudio of The Four Seasons – the Brian Wilson of New Jersey – turned the song into a strangely compelling Beach Boys-styled number for Frankie Valli to sing, and took it into the US Top 10.

A decade on, Gloria Gaynor turned it into a dance-floor

banger, perhaps truer to the original spirit of the song than any of the other versions, in that – as with so many Cole Porter songs – the glamour and lights of the disco could not conceal the emptiness and lovelessness of the song's narrator.

'I've Got You Under My Skin' will likely never die. Other songs, just as good, just as popular at the time, have already faded. That's proof not just that a song is dependent on its singer, but that only when that singer comes to encapsulate something greater does the song itself achieve transcendence. Cole Porter may have written 'I've Got You Under My Skin', but Frank Sinatra made it.

Michael Hann

THE FIRST TIME EVER I SAW YOUR FACE

47

If ever a musician were opposed to the notion of success, it was the folk singer Ewan MacColl. A proud socialist who led the 1960s folk revival in Britain, MacColl saw mainstream pop music as part of a capitalist conspiracy, and fame as an affront to artistic integrity. So when a friend called to tell him he'd heard Roberta Flack's 1972 version of his song 'The First Time Ever I Saw Your Face' played on mainstream radio, MacColl was unimpressed. When, a year later, it beat Don McLean's 'American Pie' to win Best Song at the Grammys, he was horrified. 'I was in my mid-fifties and had lived hand to mouth for almost all of my life,' he grumbled in his autobiography, *Journeyman*. 'Fame and fortune [never] figured in any of my dreams.'

MacColl had written the song in 1957 for the American singer Peggy Seeger, who would become his third wife. Seeger was in the US at the time and had requested a love song to help her flesh out a show she was planning in Los Angeles. MacColl obliged and, after finishing it, called her up and sang it down the phone.

Were it not for Clint Eastwood, who, 14 years later, was gathering tracks for his stalker film *Play Misty for Me*, the song might have been forgotten. But it wasn't Seeger's live version that caught his ear, nor the squeaky-clean 1962 recording by

San Francisco's The Kingston Trio, who exchanged the words 'the first time ever I lay with you' for 'the first time ever I held you near' to spare the listener's blushes. It was Flack's, whose elegantly understated arrangement and hymn-like delivery transformed the song into an enduring ballad not just for new lovers but also for new mothers fresh from the delivery room.

A classical pianist turned nightclub singer, Flack had recorded it in 1969 for her debut album, *First Take*, though it wasn't until Eastwood alighted on it to accompany an alfresco sex scene in *Play Misty for Me* between him and his co-star Donna Mills that it took flight. The film sparked such a demand that Atlantic records released the song as a single (edited down to four minutes from five) that subsequently went to Number 1 for six weeks.

Since then the covers have run into the hundreds by everyone from earnest folkies (Peter, Paul and Mary, Christy Moore), to old crooners (Val Doonican, Engelbert Humperdinck) and show-boating talent-show contestants (Leona Lewis, Matt Cardle).

If MacColl disapproved of Flack's cover – Seeger recently complained: 'It milked the song, especially the ending. Ewan wrote it as an hors d'oeuvre and it got turned into an entrée' – he reserved a special ire for Elvis's 1972 rendition, which he is alleged to have said sounded like Romeo at the bottom of London's Post Office Tower bellowing up to Juliet. One can only imagine what he would have made of the cast of *Glee*'s rendering in 2012, all histrionic harmonies and blustering orchestral flourishes.

That few of its interpreters have matched Flack's take on the song, still broadly viewed as the definitive version, is doubtless due to their insistence on copying rather than reimagining – though Johnny Cash went some way towards breaking the mould

on his 2002 album *American IV: The Man Comes Around*, when his craggy, 60-a-day vocals injected it with a rare dose of grit.

Perhaps the most unusual reconfiguration has come from Seeger herself, who in 2012, aged 77, recorded it alongside the electronic producer Broadcaster. MacColl's melody was all but dispensed with, Seeger's voice was fed through a vocoder and the song was set against a Gary Numan-esque synth groove. Asked what her late husband would have thought of it, Seeger replied, 'Well, the Ewan of the Seventies would have thrown it in the fire. But the Ewan of the Eighties was coming to terms with a lot of things . . . I think he would have been very interested in it.'

Fiona Sturges

48

EVERYTHING I OWN

It has been crooned so often to a warm Jamaican rhythm that it would be easy to assume that it has always been a reggae song. 'Everything I Own' is seen as one of the great romantic ballads of the 1970s, expressing emotional loss in a tender, undemonstrative way. It appears straightforward: boy loses the love of his life, expresses deep regret, longs for her return.

However, there is more to 'Everything I Own' than that. The song was written by David Gates, the singer of Bread, a group who were airbrushed from rock history because they were never hip or rebellious. Instead the quartet relied on Gates's winning way with melodies and lyrics. 'Make It With You', 'If', 'Baby I'm-a Want You' – these songs were part of pop's furniture during the early 1970s. Bread? They made plenty; a compilation, *The Best Of*, shifted 5 million copies in the US alone.

One of their hits was 'Everything I Own', which rose to Number 5 in the US charts in 1972. It didn't do so well in the UK, but the song's success was just beginning. Five months after its US release, genial middle-of-the-road TV star Andy Williams covered it. Barbara Mason, a Philadelphia soul singer, sang it, as did southern soul belter Oscar Toney Jr. In 1973, Shirley Bassey tried it on for size, but her version, in which she threw every decibel she owned at it, went unreleased for two decades.

'Everything I Own' started its unlikely parallel life as a reggae classic when Lloyd Charmers, a Jamaican record producer, suggested to one of his clients, Ken Boothe, that the song would suit him. Boothe, one of the most expressive singers in reggae, delivered it beautifully, holding back the power in his voice to produce a spine-tingling intimacy. Charmers' arrangement, with tinkling glockenspiel and mournful, brass band-like horns, matched it perfectly. Boothe actually sings 'anything I own' several times in the song, perhaps suggesting, having risen from the Denham Town ghetto in Kingston, Jamaica, that he wasn't prepared to abandon all his hard-won chattels for love. Nobody minded this reticence: his cover hit Number 1 in the UK and 'Everything I Own' was reborn.

Taking Boothe's version as his template, Boy George remade it in 1987, and it became his only solo UK chart-topper. Jason Mraz and Chrissie Hynde melded it with The Steve Miller Band's 'The Joker' for the 2006 children's film *Happy Feet*, and that same year, Rod Stewart growled it on one of his numerous albums of covers.

There have been interpretations galore but curiously, every one has been a misinterpretation. 'Everything I Own' was never a romantic ballad – not in the boy-meets-girl sense. Gates said that a friend approached him at his father's funeral and told him: 'Your father was so proud of what you were doing.' This so touched Gates that he decided to pay tribute to his father in song. The lyrics make perfect sense in that context: 'You sheltered me from harm, kept me warm, kept me warm. You gave my life to me, set me free . . .' The love Gates had been missing was parental, not romantic.

Ian McCann

49

I FOUGHT THE LAW

Some songs capture the zeitgeist in just a few words. Such was the case when Sonny Curtis, a first-generation rock'n'roller and a member of Buddy Holly's group The Crickets after Holly's death, came up with the irresistible couplet 'I fought the law, and the law won.'

Curtis's song 'I Fought the Law' went on to become a classic rebel yell of rock via The Bobby Fuller Four, and then again in the punk era thanks to The Clash. It remains a set text for almost any aspiring guitar-based combo, and has been recorded dozens of times and associated with real-life tragedy and crime along the way.

Yet for some years, it lay in relative obscurity as an album track. 'I Fought the Law' was first recorded by The Crickets, on the album they completed after Holly's 1959 death in a plane crash at the age of just 22. *In Style With the Crickets*, which became widely admired by rock'n'roll devotees as a seminal LP, contained other Curtis compositions including 'More Than I Can Say', which became a hit for teen pin-up Bobby Vee.

On 'I Fought the Law', Curtis conjures a simple but effective crime-doesn't-pay scenario of a man who needed money. His brief reign of lawlessness, 'Robbin' people with a six-gun', ends with his incarceration and ruthless punishment: even as the song opens, he is forlornly breaking rocks in the hot sun. To make things worse, he's lost his girl along the way. A cautionary tale indeed.

But even with its appealing energy, and Curtis playing forceful guitar in Holly's stead, The Crickets' original was never released as the A-side of a 45. In 1961, it was further demoted to mere flipside status, of 'A Sweet Love', the final single from the album *In Style With the Crickets*. Another year on, a version by Paul Stefen and the Royal Lancers became successful in their home town of Milwaukee, but failed to trouble the compilers of nationwide charts.

Late in 1965, however, 'I Fought the Law' didn't just get out on parole, it was given a full pardon. It was revived by The Bobby Fuller Four, who were starting to gain attention beyond their origins in El Paso, Texas, fronted by a young man who had already been releasing independent singles for four years. 'I Fought the Law' had long been a trademark of their live shows, and after an all-night recording session, it was released as a single and blew up on radio stations across the US.

In the UK, it only scraped into the Top 40, but it did have some notable British admirers: in an interview in early 1966, George Harrison said The Bobby Fuller Four were his most listened-to group.

Fuller was to die in never-explained circumstances, found in a petrol-soaked car a few months later, aged just 23. The cause of death, first described, improbably, as suicide, was later changed to accidental. His flagship version of 'I Fought the Law' would live on: the song was covered in the 1970s by Roy Orbison, as a B-side by Tom Petty and the Heartbreakers and, perhaps most incongruously, as a duet by Kris Kristofferson and Rita Coolidge.

Then, in the summer of 1978, Joe Strummer and Mick Jones

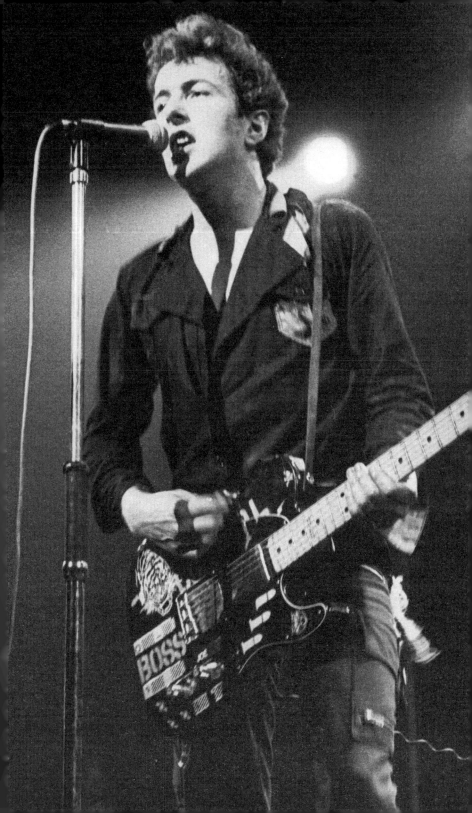

of The Clash were in San Francisco, recording overdubs for the band's second album *Give 'Em Enough Rope*. Hanging out at the Automatt studio, and pumping the house jukebox with quarters, they played Fuller's single repeatedly. Such was its impact that they were moved to cut the song with The Clash for the band's 1979 EP 'The Cost of Living'. It remains one of their best-loved and most-aired tracks.

The song has since been revived as a Green Day single, a Pogues B-side and on a Bryan Adams live album. In 1987, punk figureheads The Dead Kennedys recorded it in memory of an infamous double killing in 1978 in which San Francisco politician Dan White shot and killed the city's mayor George Moscone and supervisor Harvey Milk. White was subsequently convicted of manslaughter, rather than first-degree murder, and the band changed the lyric to: 'I blew George and Harvey's brains out with my six-gun! I fought the law and I won', thoroughly subverting Sonny Curtis's enduring tale of ill-starred rebellion.

Paul Sexton

YOU'LL NEVER WALK ALONE

Many popular songs have made their way on to the football terraces of the world, but perhaps the best known of these is 'You'll Never Walk Alone'. For more than 50 years, it has been sung by football fans around the globe – at Liverpool FC, whose fans are its best-known champions, and also at Glasgow Celtic, Borussia Dortmund, Feyenoord and FC Tokyo. Its avowal of solidarity in the face of adversity provides a tonic for the vicissitudes of the beautiful game.

The song was written by Richard Rodgers and Oscar Hammerstein II for their 1945 musical *Carousel*. It is sung twice during the show, the second time in the climactic graduation scene, when Louise realizes that she does not have to live as an outcast. The song quickly attracted accolades – Irving Berlin compared it to the 23rd Psalm. First recorded in 1945 by the Broadway cast, it was soon covered by Frank Sinatra, who released it as a single. The film version of the musical in 1956 took the song to a wider audience. It was recorded by artists as diverse as rock'n'roller Gene Vincent and Doris Day.

In 1963, Liverpool band Gerry and the Pacemakers were cresting the Merseybeat wave. They were managed by Beatles manager Brian Epstein and produced by George Martin at Abbey Road. They'd scored their first Number 1 with Mitch Murray's 'How Do You Do It', a song The Beatles had rejected in favour of their own 'Please Please Me'. Another Murray composition, 'I Like It', provided a second Number 1. Emboldened, Gerry Marsden's band dismissed the advice of Epstein and Martin and rejected John Lennon and Paul McCartney's 'Hello Little Girl' as their next single in favour of 'You'll Never Walk Alone', which also went to Number 1. ('Hello Little Girl', spurned by The Beatles, became a hit for another Liverpool group in Epstein's stable, The Fourmost.)

In those days, Top 10 singles were played over the public address system at Liverpool FC's ground, Anfield, and the crowd would sing along. After Gerry and the Pacemakers' 'You'll Never Walk Alone' dropped out of the Top 10, the fans kept singing it and adopted it as the unofficial club anthem. In 1964 the Liverpool team sang it alongside Gerry and the Pacemakers on *The Ed Sullivan Show*, and the following year the club's manager Bill Shankly included the song among his Desert Island Discs on the BBC radio show.

Elvis Presley recorded it in 1967, a homage to his boyhood idol, the singer Roy Hamilton, whose soulful version in 1954 was his breakthrough hit. Roy Orbison recorded it in 1969 in a similar arrangement to his 1961 hit 'Running Scared' – another song that built to an emotional climax over a bolero rhythm.

Pink Floyd wove samples from a field recording of Liverpool fans singing the anthem into their song 'Fearless', from their 1971 album *Meddle*. It provides a stirring coda after the final line, when the subject of the song rises above his fears, looks down and hears 'the sound of the faces in the crowd'.

As rock music expanded into arenas and stadiums, the song moved with it. In May 1977, Queen played at the Bingley Hall in Stafford. The group's guitarist Brian May told the BBC: 'We did an encore and then went off. Instead of just keeping clapping, [the crowd] sang "You'll Never Walk Alone" to us, and we were just completely knocked out.' May says that Queen classics such as 'We Will Rock You' and 'We Are the Champions' were 'in some way connected' with the experience of hearing their fans singing 'You'll Never Walk Alone'.

'You'll Never Walk Alone' took on a fresh resonance in the 1980s. In 1985, Marsden and McCartney were among the contributors to a charity cover version to raise funds for victims of the Bradford City stadium fire. It was also adopted as an anthem by survivors and campaigners after the 1989 Hillsborough disaster, in which 96 Liverpool fans died.

In 'You'll Never Walk Alone', Rodgers and Hammerstein penned the ultimate show-stopper, a modern hymn whose ripples still reverberate around rock concerts and football stadiums.

Jon Dennis

INDEX

PHOTO CREDITS

1 The Monkees: (top) Peter Tork and Mickey Dolenz, (bottom) David Jones and Mike Nesmith, 1966; © Bettmann/Getty images

2 Kate Bush performing Wuthering Heights in 1978; © Pictorial Press Ltd / Alamy Stock Photo

4 Randy Meisner, Don Felder and Joe Walsh, of The Eagles, onstage during the 'Hotel California' tour, 1977; © Richard E. Aaron/Redferns/Getty Images

6 Jack White and Meg White, February 2002; © Tim Roney/ Hulton Archive/ Getty Images

8 Ray Charles recording in the studio, c.1960; © Michael Ochs Archives/Getty Images

10 Bobbie Gentry appearing on *The Perry Como Holiday Special*, 1967; © Everett Collection Inc / Alamy Stock Photo

11 Agnetha Fältskog (left) and Anni-Frid Lyngstad (right) of ABBA performing at Radio City Music Hall, New York, 2 October 1979; © Lewton Cole / Alamy Stock Photo

13 Bryan Ferry performing at Wembley Arena, 1980; © Brian Rasic/Hulton Archive/Getty Images

14 Screamin' Jay Hawkins, 1960; © Charlie Gillett/Redferns/ Getty Images

17 Jimmy Forrest poses for Triumph Records on 21 May 1959,

in NYC; © Donaldson Collection/Michael Ochs Archives/ Getty Images

19 Carly Simon onstage, c.1972; © Michael Ochs Archives/ Getty Images

22 Jimi Hendrix performing at the Marquee Club, London, 1967; © MARC SHARRAT/REX/Shutterstock

23 Cyndi Lauper, mid 1980s © Bill Marino/Sygma via Getty Images

24 Ian Curtis and Bernard Sumner performing at Bowdon Vale Youth Club, UK, 14 March 1979; © Martin O'Neill/Redferns/ Getty Images

26 Ella Fitzgerald performing at 'Mr Kelly's' nightclub, Chicago, 1958; © Yale Joel/The LIFE Picture Collection/Getty Images

27 The Shirelles: Beverley Lee, Doris Kenner-Jackson, Shirley Alston and Addie 'Micki' Harris, 1961; © Gilles Petard/ Redferns/ Getty Images

29 Gloria Jones, June 1976; © Michael Putland/Hulton Archive/ Getty Images

32 Sheet music cover image of 'It's a Long Way to Tipperary', 1912; © Sheridan Libraries/Levy/Gado/Getty Images

34 Dolly Parton at the Glastonbury Festival, 2014; © WENN Ltd / Alamy Stock Photo

36 Lou Reed, c.1973; © Michael Ochs Archives/Getty Images

37 Amy Winehouse arriving at the Earls Court Arena, ahead of the BRIT Awards, 14 February 2007; © Leon Neal/AFP/ Getty Images

39 TLC: Rozonda 'Chilli' Thomas, Tionne 'T-Boz' Watkins and Lisa 'Left Eye' Lopes, c.1999; © ZUMA Press, Inc. / Alamy Stock Photo

41 Massive Attack: Robert del Naja, Grant Marshall and Andrew Vowles, 1998; © Everett Collection Inc / Alamy Stock Photo

44 Todd Duncan and Anne Brown in an early production of *Porgy and Bess;* © Bettmann/Getty Images

47 Roberta Flack, performing at the Newport Jazz Festival, Newport, Rhode Island, USA, 2 July 1971; © David Redfern/ Redferns/Getty Images

49 Mick Jones and Joe Strummer of The Clash performing at The Roxy, Harlesden, London, 25 October 1978; © Gus Stewart/Redferns/Getty Images